PURE
BLISS

GILL EDWARDS

PURE BLISS

The art of living in Soft Time

PIATKUS

To John –
for the pure bliss
we share together.

For more information on other books published by Piatkus, visit our website
at www.piatkus.co.uk

First published in the UK by
Judy Piatkus (Publishers) Limited
5 Windmill Street
London W1P 1HF
e-mail: info@piatkus.co.uk

The moral right of the author has been asserted

*A catalogue record for this book is available
from the British Library*

ISBN 0 7499 2052 1

Page design by Sue Ryall

Typeset by Action Publishing Technology Ltd, Gloucester
Printed and bound in Great Britain by
Biddles Ltd, Guildford & King's Lynn

Contents

This is the time of union,

the time of eternal beauty.

It is the time of luck and kindness;

It is the ocean of purity.

The wave of bestowal has come.

The roar of the sea is here.

The morning of happiness has dawned.

RUMI[1]

BLISS: Great but quiet enjoyment; heavenly joy; perfect happiness.

Old English: bliths

Foreword

Meandering down a grassy cliff path in warm sunshine, with our excited toddler in a backpack, we emerge on a long sandy beach speckled with seashells. The three of us play piggyback and chase each other, laughing and tumbling in the warm sand, splashing our feet in rippling waves, exploring curvy shells and pastel pebbles, sharing fruit juice and chocolate, 'as happy as the day is long'. Across the sparkling water lie the mountains of the Mull of Kintyre, evocative and mysterious in the summer haze. A wild otter appears at the water's edge, just a stone's throw away from us, and sleepily sunbathes for a while before vanishing into the sea – emerging minutes later with a fish, which he gobbles between both paws like a ravenous child. We watch – entranced and delighted by this rare and magical scene. It feels like a gift.

I am on holiday with my family on the Scottish isle of Arran. It is a week of warm sunny weather – and we have a heavenly time amidst seals and otters and eagles, pottering around sleepy villages, visiting standing stones, watching brightly coloured fishing-boats and walking for sundrenched miles along deserted country lanes and beautiful coastal paths.

In the midst of this glorious week of 'Soft Time', while spending a couple of hours alone on Holy Island, the idea for this book bubbles up quite unexpectedly. Before we leave Arran, I find I have written the synopsis, almost without realising it. (It is a complete surprise, since I had planned to write for children next.) As I muse upon it, I realise that I need to share the ideas about living in Soft Time which have emerged from several years of reflecting, experimenting and 'simply being', during a time of gentle transformation in my own life. The more I think about it, the more excited and passionate I feel . . . This book is the result.

Until recent years, I spent most of my adult life being over-busy and over-committed. I always loved my work – first as a writer and clinical psychologist, then as a spiritual teacher – but I couldn't seem to get my life into balance. My personal life was often non-existent, since there was little space for 'me' in my schedule. Gradually I observed that I seemed to switch between two different time cycles. One cycle felt exhausting and fairly fruitless, while the other was creative and joyful.

The first cycle – what I call living in Hard Time – felt like a downward spiral, full of struggle, 'efforting' and busywork. It felt heavy and cluttered. There were diary-packed stretches of over-commitment which felt rushed and pressurising, punctuated by periods of attempted recovery or 'relaxation' which were empty and frustrating. I felt like a hamster treading a wheel – trying harder and harder to get who-knows-where, and always falling short. I felt disembodied and disconnected. I was often tense, anxious or guilt-ridden, and yet efforts to 'try even harder' or catch up on the backlog just seemed to make things worse. Despite all this, Hard Time had an addictive quality which kept hooking me back in.

The second cycle – living in Soft Time – was a different, almost timeless world. It involved intensely creative and fulfilling periods when everything seemed to flow, when I felt inspired, heart-centred and soul-ful – along with blissful periods of simply relaxing and being-in-the-moment. Life seemed much simpler, and yet far richer.

As I became more aware of these two cycles in my own life, I began to wonder what the secret was to living in Soft Time. I slowly became aware of the 'hooks' which pulled me back into Hard Time, and discovered ways of shifting – sometimes instantly – from one time cycle to the other. Eventually I found that I stayed in Soft Time almost permanently – and as I stopped *trying* so hard and being so busy-busy, my life was gradually transformed. My outer life changed to reflect my new contentment: I moved to the heart of the Lake District, fell in love, married and (at the age of 41) became a mother.

I felt pretty sure that these two time-cycles, or states of awareness, were universal – and that anyone who was having a Hard Time could learn to live in Soft Time instead.

Sure enough, when I began to teach the concepts in my *Living Magically* workshops, people quickly identified with these two modes of being – and began to use the ideas in their everyday lives.

There are difficult periods in everyone's life, and *some* stress – such as that of bereavement – is an unavoidable part of being human. However, the vast majority of our stress is self-created and unnecessary. It comes from living in Hard Time. It saps our energy, distracts us from our higher purpose, makes us fuss and fret about trivia, and blocks our enjoyment of life – and if we make life difficult for ourselves, it also rebounds on our family, friends and everyone around us.

When we live in Soft Time, life's challenges become much more worthwhile and positive. We feel more present and alive. We tap into our inner wisdom with ease. We are more focused and creative, and perform at our peak – whatever the task. Work feels like play. Life seems simple, unhurried and carefree. We live in wonder and delight. We are always in the right place at the right time – and everyday life is full of joy and delight.

In Soft Time, enough is enough and less is more. It feels uplifting and deeply satisfying, yet almost effortless. It is a song of the soul. There is room to breathe and space to move and dance. Living in Soft Time also releases our true potential. It means we live a *meaningful* and *purposeful* life – a life that really makes a difference. The world of Soft Time is an upward, expanding spiral. It is 'living in the 4th dimension'. It is heaven on earth.

In **Part One**, I describe what it means to live in the cycles of Hard Time and Soft Time – and why most of us get stuck in Hard Time. In **Part Two**, I offer 70 guidelines for putting the theory into practice, and becoming a 'natural mystic': how to apply the principles to your inner Self, relationships, parenting, work, money, health and home. Of course, living in Soft Time is not something we can 'do' by following a 'cookbook guide'. It is a state of consciousness, a form of being-ness, something we might slip into while we're not watching – so a self-help guide on 'how to do it' might seem paradoxical. The paradox is resolved when we remember that 'the steps to getting there are the qualities of being there'. In other words, by acting *as if* you have already achieved something, *as if* you are already your future self, you begin to become that person. By taking on the qualities, actions and awareness of a natural mystic, you begin to 'be there', more and more of the time – until it becomes as effortless as breathing.

As I write this foreword, I pause to gaze dreamily from our leaded windows at the Lakeland landscape: soaring fells glistening in the autumn sunshine, trees aflame with red, gold and burnished copper. Suddenly my husband John peeps around the door – and our toddler rushes up to me in a giggling flurry of little limbs. I wrap him in my arms and kiss his golden halo of curls. John sits down eager to share his news, and we decide to stroll down to Rydal Water in time for the sunset. I feel so blessed, and am filled with waves of gratitude. Life is pure bliss. And surely it was always meant to be this way.

PART ONE

1
Hard Time, Soft Time and the Flow

I am not this steeply sloping hour in which you see me hurrying.
RAINER MARIA RILKE

IMAGINE A PICNIC on a grassy riverbank on a hazy summer's day. Generous remains of bread, cheese, shiny red apples, rich fruit cake and wine are spread on a white linen table-cloth beside a huge wicker hamper. Dreamy conversation and gentle laughter drifts through the air. People doze in the warm sunshine, straw hats of pale yellow tipped across their faces. Others glide effortlessly past in wooden rowing boats, oars dipping occasionally into the water, carried by the river's flow. The scent of wild flowers hangs in the warm languid air. It is a glorious, heavenly day which feels as if it might last forever.

Or imagine young children playing in a huge garden filled with secret passageways, sweeping lawns and rope swings; running and chasing and giggling; clambering on gnarled and ancient trees; stopping in wonder to gaze at a purple flower or a shiny black beetle. It is a timeless day when nothing seems to matter – or even seems real – except play, laughter, joy and delight.

This is what I call Soft Time – living in the moment, feeling happy and carefree. It is a world of soft focus and pastel hues. There are no jarring notes, no jagged edges, nothing to disturb; no conflicts, worries or concerns; no thoughts of past or future. There is no goal, no purpose. There is just the eternal *now*.

When we're in Soft Time, we might feel intense joy at catching a falling leaf, seeing a pale wintry sun, hearing a child laugh or a skylark sing, or stroking the mossy bark of a tree. We feel whole and complete. We feel connected. Our mind is peaceful and still. There is no desire to search, to act, to do. Everything we need is right here – in *this* moment. Soft Time is 'recreation' in its true sense – time in which we re-create the Self by coming back to ourselves, by deeply relaxing, by simply 'being' for a while. It is a space for reflection and inte-gration. In its highest form, Soft Time is the place of mystical experience, of expanded awareness, of oneness with nature. It is a place of coming home to our souls.

Soft Time might mean 'just sitting' in a garden, or walking in the woods, or soaking in the bath, or reading poetry, or going to an art gallery, or listening (*really listening*) to music, or watching butterflies dance, or seeing morning mist slowly fade as the sun rises, or gazing into the eyes of your loved one, or meditating, or simply doing nothing. Or it might mean something more active such as horse-riding, meeting a friend for coffee or going to a funfair. The point is that there is no point to it! It is goal-less time – purely for pleasure – when you live in the moment.

Of course, we cannot live forever in the pure being-ness of

Soft Time. We have to balance 'being' with 'doing' – making decisions, letting go, moving on, learning and growing and changing. That is the nature of life, of being human. *Soft Time is not a stuck position, but part of a flowing cycle of time.*

The pure being-ness of Soft Time allows space for reflection and integration. After a while, we shift naturally into an open, receptive state of mind. As we 'follow our energy', doing whatever we feel moved to do – perhaps gently pottering, cleaning, gardening, decorating or just sitting – we remain quiet and unhurried, and open to deep stirrings from our soul. Since we're deeply relaxed and at peace with ourselves, we are sensitive to the 'still small voice within', the gentle promptings of our soul. We might reflect on issues, decisions or ongoing projects – and without any effort, we receive fresh insights, inspiration or guidance. In time, it feels easy and natural to move back into action, 'knowing' the next steps to take . . . .

The ecstasy of Flow Time

Once we intuitively 'know' what choices to make, or action to take – and the timing feels right – we move into the active phase of the Soft Time cycle. This is a timeless space where we are living in perfect balance within ourselves, and are connected with the Source, the Tao, the Mystery, the Great Spirit, the universal force. It is often known as 'being in the flow'. Athletes call it 'the zone' – the state of mind where they reach peak performance. It is a place where real magic happens.

When you're in Flow Time, everything seems easy and effortless. There is no inner conflict, no struggle, no fear or doubt – and your inner harmony is mirrored in the outer world. Meaningful coincidences – what Jung called 'synchronicities' – are commonplace. You are always in the right place at the right time. Invisible hands seem to open every door as you approach. You 'happen' to bump into the very person you need to see. Parking spaces appear just when you need them. You buy a certain newspaper for the first time, and it holds an advert for your ideal job. You decide to sell your home, pop into a local café – unusually for you – and bump into a stranger who wants to buy your house. You choose some garden furniture from a brochure, and phone to find it has been reduced to half-price that day. It feels as if the angels are on your side, supporting your every move.

Everything we do in Flow Time gushes forth like a mountain spring. The project which felt such a heavy struggle before is suddenly completed with astonishing ease. The difficult letter which you avoided for several weeks is dealt with simply in a few minutes. You make up a bedtime story for your child which begins as a traditional tale – but as it unfolds from your imagination, you develop an exhilarating sense that it is coming from somewhere else, that it is emerging *through* you rather than *from* you. You pass into a timeless, eternal world – and are as intrigued as your child as the story continues.

A tennis player who slips into 'the zone' sees the ball as huge, and travelling in slow motion – as if there is endless time to decide upon their return shot, position themselves, and hit a winner. Concentration is total. Player, racquet, ball have become a poetic unity. Trying to beat the other player is no longer the aim; instead there is a sense of allowing perfection to unfold for its own sake, competing only with oneself, stretching to the limit for the sheer joy of it. It might only last for a game, set – or just for one breathtaking shot – but the experience of being in the flow is ecstatic.

Dwell as near as possible to the channel in which your life flows.
HENRY DAVID THOREAU

In Flow Time, we are paradoxically both goal-less (living in the moment) *and* goal-directed (moving towards our Dreams or visions). We are aware of our uniqueness *and* we feel at One with our goal or activity, as if our boundaries have become softer and fuzzier. Our masculine and feminine energies are in balance and harmony. (The terms 'masculine' and 'feminine' have little to do with whether we are male or female; they are simply a way of describing our 'masculine' drive towards individuality or separateness and our 'feminine' pull towards merging, unity, oneness.)

Many of us imagine that it would be pure bliss to lie on a tropical beach all day sipping cocktails, with nothing busier to do than apply fresh layers of suntan lotion. However, research on the psychology of happiness suggests that we are *not* happiest while relaxing. The traditional Christian notion of heaven – with angels playing harps and 'everlasting rest in peace' – would be sheer hell for most of us. In reality, we tend to feel most joyful while we are *totally immersed in reaching for a challenging goal which we have chosen ourselves* – any heartfelt goal which involves building our knowledge, skills and awareness, or developing our personal strengths.[1]

Everyone needs to have Dreams to reach for – not winning the lottery, which is usually a fantasy about *escaping* from everyday life, but real, challenging, heart-centred Dreams which you are prepared to act upon and turn into reality, such as finding work that you love, meeting your life partner, creating a beautiful home, having vibrant health, writing a novel, becoming a sculptor, winning a golf championship, giving birth to a child, setting up your own business . . . . When you are *living* your Dreams – not waiting to reach your goal, but loving the moment-by-moment process of making those Dreams come true – you will be in the Flow.

Flow Time is energising and exhilarating – but after a while, we need to slow down and integrate our new experience. We need time to reflect, time to relax, time to balance and re-centre ourselves – and to enjoy the simple pleasures of life, without any aim or purpose. And so we move into the goal-less phase of Soft Time again – and the cycle continues.

Flow Time and Soft Time feed and support each other. When we are living our Dreams, it is much easier to relax and enjoy being in the moment. I was recently blowing bubbles at midnight with my toddler, who was unexpectedly wide-awake at a time when I had planned to write. I noticed that I was hugely enjoying our game, and not fretting at all about my missed writing session. I had written a satisfying chunk earlier that day, while he had a snooze – and 'enough is enough' in Soft Time – so I was utterly content to have midnight frolics with my son.

Similarly, Soft Time feeds Flow Time. It is when we slow down and quiet our minds in Soft Time that we become open and receptive, and receive the guidance and inspiration which leads us into Flow Time. The Soft Time cycle is self-perpetuating; it is a 'virtuous cycle' which leads upwards and upwards – towards more joy and ease, more creativity, more freedom, more clarity, more simplicity, more fulfilment.

Theoretically one can find joy in the moment *whatever* our situation (even in a concentration camp, as Viktor Frankl[2] so poignantly described). There is the well-known story of the

Zen Buddhist monk who is chased over a cliff by a tiger – and as he hangs from a collapsing vine over the cliff edge, facing certain death, he sees a strawberry just within his reach. He plucks and eats it. It tastes *very* good! Whatever one's situation, there is always the beauty of nature, sensual pleasures, the joy of loving, or the miracle of being alive to enjoy. It is always possible to shift into Soft Time, and find peace and joy in the moment. But if the monk had been in the Flow, would he have found himself in the tiger's path in the first place?

Flow Time ensures we are in the right place at the right time, and tends to improve our quality of life – while the 'being-ness' of Soft Time allows us to appreciate and enjoy that greater quality of life. Together, Flow Time and Soft Time help us to create heaven on earth.

We might move through the Soft Time cycle several times in the course of a day, or even in a few minutes. Soft Time and Flow Time can be a seamless shifting of energy: relaxing, creating, daydreaming, working, gazing out of the window. There are also cycles within cycles. We might follow the rhythms of nature, being more reflective and quiet during the autumn months, seeking inspiration and guidance during winter, moving into the flow on projects in spring and summer – writing that radio play, converting the garage into an office, landscaping the garden, setting up a recycling project – then scaling down our commitments again for the autumn. Or summer might be our natural time to relax and reflect on life. We might need a long quiet period of incubation for a particular creative project; and we might have even longer cycles – such as having two or three 'busy' years at work, followed by a deliberately quiet year in which we take stock and integrate all our new experiences before moving on.

Being busy doesn't necessarily mean you are in Hard Time. If you are 'following your bliss' and living in the moment, then you are in Soft Time – even if you choose to be busy for a while. Part of living in Soft Time is getting to know your own natural rhythms, and being alert to signals from your body or inner Self that you need to slow down, or take action, or simply 'be' for a while; if you ignore these signs, you slip into Hard Time.

Living in Soft Time (or Hard Time) is not an all-or-none affair. Most of us shift in and out of both cycles, sometimes several times a day. Some people are in Soft Time around some issues in their life, such as work, health or family – but find that certain people, or shopping in a supermarket, or thinking about money always shifts them into Hard Time. Others find that they can stay in Soft Time for a few days at a time, or for a while after a holiday, but keep getting hooked back into Hard Time.

The struggle of Hard Time

The cycle of Hard Time is like living on a different planet. It is a world in which life is a struggle for survival, there is always far too much to do in too little time, and it all feels rather empty and meaningless. There is no room for singing and dancing and celebrating – and even if there were, your heart would not be in it.

Hard Time is the polar opposite of Soft Time. When you're living in Hard Time, you feel hurried and pressurised. You are forever clock-watching, often working to tight deadlines or packing your days with appointments, so that you're running to catch up with yourself. You are tense and unable to relax. Your energy feels scattered. You feel overwhelmed by demands and obligations, as if the world is crowding in on you. Your life, your head, your home is cluttered. Your hours are filled with 'busy-work' – trivial, meaningless and unsatisfying tasks which somehow feel necessary – because you have lost sight of what really matters to you (or have never even asked yourself what your Dreams and priorities are). Despite dashing about all day, you never seem to do anything worthwhile.

When you're having a Hard Time, you focus on the past or the future – mulling over conversations you had yesterday, or regrets about the past, or thinking anxiously about where you have to be next, what else needs to be done, or what might happen. You are never fully present *right now*. Living is often something that will happen in the future: when the kids go to school, when you're fully qualified, when this project is over, when the house is finished, when you're less tired, when you're financially secure, when you find the right partner, when you have a new job, when the children are grown up, some mythical day 'when you have more time'. Life in Hard Time is a matter of survival, of getting through the day, of waiting for the good times to come.

Despite this, there is an addictive quality to Hard Time. We can get high on the adrenaline rush of dashing about with a sense of urgency, or meeting deadlines, or being busy-busy. We can also kid ourselves that being busy means being valued and 'important' – and we might fear what would happen if we slowed down enough to get in touch with ourselves. Being busy is a great way of avoiding our emotions, avoiding intimacy, avoiding messages from our deep Self, avoiding being fully alive.

Chronic Hard Timers rarely, if ever, go on holiday – and if they do, they are easily 'bored' and find it difficult to relax. They dash about to a packed timetable, keep glancing at their watches and generally look harassed. ('If this is Tuesday, it must be Paris!') Some keep their adrenaline levels high by engaging in dangerous sports and pastimes on holiday. Others lie on a sunbed with their mobile phone and laptop within easy reach, as if they are terrified of being on holiday, and secretly wish they were somewhere reassuringly busy and demanding.

Our addictive culture encourages us to live in Hard Time – to rush, to fill our lives with trivia, to aim to 'have' and 'do' more and more. It gives us no sense of meaning or purpose. So we compulsively buy more and more in the fantasy that if we *have* enough we will be happy, or jam-pack our diaries until there is no room to breathe, in the fantasy that if only we *do* enough, we will feel fulfilled. But enough never feels enough – so we try even harder, hurry more, buy more, do more, and *still* happiness seems to lie around the next corner. The word 'enough' makes no sense when we're in Hard Time. We have no concept of balance. We think only in linear terms. We always want *more*.

Lost Time and the addictive cycle

It is stressful and tiring to live in Hard Time. Sooner or later, we feel the urge to relax and have some 'down time' to recover. Feeling stressed out – and wanting to do something about it – leads us into the more 'passive' phase of the Hard Time cycle: Lost Time.

The problem is that 'relaxing' is not restorative when you

are stuck in Hard Time. It doesn't reconnect you with your Self. It often means watching mindless TV, playing computer games, shopping, gossiping with friends, or aimlessly surfing the Internet – keeping your mind 'occupied' so that you can ignore the silent scream of your soul. Or it means lying on a beach with trashy novels for a fortnight to 'recover' a little from your over-busy life before returning to the treadmill. This is Lost Time – wasted time which neither restores balance and brings us home to ourselves, nor gives us any real joy. (How many people feel *joy* while watching angst-ridden soap operas, or traipsing around a shopping mall?)

At best, Lost Time helps us to cope with a stressful and unfulfilling lifestyle, and to survive for another week, or month, or year (just as tranquillisers and anti-depressants often help people to 'cope' with situations which they really need to change). A tragedy of Western culture is that, despite hours of 'free time' each day, and despite saying that we want *more* leisure time, most of us waste it on joyless and mindless pursuits – because we have lost touch with our deep Self. It is impossible to appreciate the simple pleasures of life – smelling roses seems dull or pointless – since we're not really *here*. We're just going through the motions.

Lost Time leaves us feeling frustrated, anxious and empty inside. It fails to renew us, to satisfy us. We yearn even more to 'fill' ourselves in order to feel connected, to feel good, to feel whole again. This is part of the vicious cycle of addiction and co-dependency which is endemic to Western society. When we are in the Hard Time cycle, we tend to look for solutions *outside* ourselves. Since we do not allow ourselves peace, solitude and being-time to connect with our deep Self, we search for our lost wholeness in the outer world – through work, shopping, love, sex, religion, TV, sport, drugs, alcohol or just plain busyness. This gives us a 'buzz' for a little while, then we 'come down' and need another fix. The fantasy is that if we just try hard enough or wait long enough, the strategy will work – we will be happy, fulfilled, at peace – but the harder we try, the more we push away the missing parts of our Self. It is a hopeless strategy. (It reminds me of the story of the man who lost his keys one night, and was found searching beneath a lamp-post. 'Is this where you lost them?' asks a helpful passer-by. 'No', he replies, 'but the light is better here.')

The secret of pure bliss

Soft Time is a state of consciousness, not an activity (or lack of it). You cannot guarantee being in Soft Time simply by sitting in the garden 'doing nothing'. If your eyes are darting around the garden noticing the weeding and pruning and mulching that needs to be done, while you battle with yourself over whether you can afford to relax for a few minutes, then you are in Hard Time. Or if you're sitting in your garden feeling overwhelmed by your life, 'giving up' for a while from sheer exhaustion – then you will hardly be aware of the garden. Its beauty and magic will leave your heart untouched, since you are in Lost Time.

Similarly, if you are bathing a young child, you might revel in the rainbow beauty of the soap bubbles, the softness of your child's skin, the radiance of their smile, the shared laughter of a vigorous splash – and you are in the bliss of Soft Time. Alternatively, you might bathe a child while

Basic assumptions: The universe is hostile. I'm not good enough.

Feel stressed out/exhausted by treadmill
of life. Need 'down time' to recover.

HARD TIME

Busywork, 'efforting' and
addictive behaviour. Clock-
watching. Struggle, conflict and
anxiety. Feel 'driven' by duties,
obligations and tasks. Focus on
status and approval-seeking.
Defensive martyrhood and guilt.
Scattered energy. Lots of clutter
and trivia. No sense of meaning
or purpose.

HARD
TIME
CYCLE

LOST TIME

Try hard to relax, and escape.
Tend to fill or waste time,
and 'keep occupied'. Often
feel bored. Stimulation-
seeking. Joyless and mindless
pursuits.

Feel frustrated/empty/numb. Search *outside* self for happiness
and fulfilment (or merely for safety and security).

← **ACTIVE** - - - - - - - - - - - - - ↕ - - - - - - -- - - - - - - **PASSIVE** →

Natural tendency to *balance* one's life after active or
creative period: time for reflection and integration.

FLOW TIME

Free-flowing activity. Joy
and fulfilment. Clarity of
higher purpose. Sense of
freedom and fearlessness.
Highly creative and
productive. Living your
Dreams. Peak performance
and effortless concentration.
Inner peace and harmony.
'Meaningful coincidences'
are commonplace.

SOFT
TIME
CYCLE

SOFT TIME

Being-time. Living
totally in the moment,
without any goal or
purpose. Mystical
awareness. Sense of
awe, wonder and
delight. Celebration of
nature. Appreciation
and gratitude. Enjoy
simple pleasures of life.
Pure bliss.

Connect easily and naturally with inner
guidance and inspiration. Clearly see bigger
picture of your life, and next steps to take.

Basic assumptions: The universe is friendly. I am loved.

mentally listing other jobs to do, or fretting about the TV programme you are missing, telling your child to hurry up, and feeling bored or impatient. Then you're in Hard Time. It is not our actions or circumstances which determine whether we are in Hard or Soft Time; it is where we are holding our awareness.

Scientists reckon that we use only 10 per cent of our brain's capacity. I see this as our Hard Time mind, our conscious rational mind or ego-self – our '10 per cent mind' – which we normally have access to. Our '90 per cent mind' lies in Soft Time – and it carries almost limitless creative and psychic potential. When we live more in Soft Time, our thinking becomes bigger, more expansive, holistic, creative and free-flowing. We see the forest rather than the trees – and often simplify our lives accordingly.

Since Soft Time has been ignored and devalued in Western society, we vastly overuse our Hard Time mind, and give it tasks which it was not designed for – such as providing purpose or inspiration, or creative solutions to problems, or dealing with emotional issues, or simply enjoying the moment. Instead of seeing the forest, we walk slap-bang into one tree-trunk after another. It is not the fault of our ego-self; it has just been stretched beyond its limits. It was always meant to *serve* our 90 per cent mind, our deep Self – but instead it has taken charge, and set its own fast-paced but small-minded agenda.

Unless we make space for pure Soft Time in our lives – aimless pottering and idling, daydreaming, just 'being' – we never hear the inspiring voice of our soul, never get in touch with our dreams and visions, never listen to the needs of our inner Child, never notice when our intuition nudges us, never feel fully alive. And we *know* there is something missing – something heartbreakingly crucial. At best, we feel numb and slightly anxious; at worst, we feel desperate and lost without even knowing why.

It is Soft Time that whispers to us 'Enough is enough'. It is Soft Time that hints that happiness is not to be found in the latest software or going on a shopping spree, that we are more likely to find inner peace and harmony by watching a river flow, or taking our dog for a long walk. The irony is that when we stop *chasing* happiness so frantically, slow down and learn to live in the moment, we are far more likely to be joyful, creative and fulfilled – and without the struggle, 'efforting' and busywork associated with Hard Time. In Hard Time, we are like caterpillars busily and greedily trying to chomp our way towards a bright new future. In Soft Time, we are already butterflies – flying free.

Signs that you're having a Hard Time might be any of the following:

- Struggle and 'efforting'.
- Feeling tense, hurried, pressurised, 'driven'.
- Clock-watching.
- Feeling heavy and tired.
- Busywork: 'keeping busy' but not getting anything important done.
- Focusing on details and trivia; not being able to see the forest for the trees.
- Fear and anxiety.
- Shame and guilt.

- Self-pity and martyrhood.
- Attracting 'bad luck', crisis or melodrama.
- Being unable to enjoy simple pleasures of life.
- Feeling numb or joyless.
- Feeling lonely and disconnected.
- Feeling that 'something is missing', or 'there must be more to life than this'.
- Depression or apathy.
- Unwanted duties and obligations.
- Exhaustion and burnout.
- No sense of meaning or purpose.
- Feeling that life is 'one problem after another'.
- Not knowing what to do with your free time.
- Boredom and frustration.
- Feeling out of control of your life.
- Wasting time.
- Living for weekends or holidays.
- Living for the future.
- Fretting about the past.
- Getting upset over trivia.
- Losing your sense of humour.
- Losing your sense of perspective.
- Feeling trapped.
- Feeling you have too much to do in too little time.
- Looking for direction from others.
- Rapid, anxious thoughts which 'go round and round'.
- Thinking about what you have to do *next*, rather than what you're doing *now*.
- Over-concern with status and appearance.
- Approval-seeking.
- Criticising or judging self and others.

- Unequal, co-dependent relationships (e.g. compulsive caretaking, child-like neediness or avoidance of intimacy).
- Compulsively working, spending, eating, drinking, TV-watching, smoking, exercising, reading, meditating etc. (That is, using addictions to numb yourself emotionally, 'fill your emptiness' or get a false high.)
- Not enjoying your work.
- Continuing a task long after your body or inner Self says 'Stop'.
- Not having much *fun*.
- Feeling empty.
- Feeling not good enough or undeserving.
- Feeling unsafe in the world.
- Your home or office being full of clutter.
- Losing your sense of awe and wonder at nature.
- Feeling restless and anxious.
- Being easily distracted, with scattered energy.
- Waking up with that 'Monday morning feeling'.

Signs that you are in the Soft Time cycle:

- Feeling happy and fulfilled.
- Living in the moment.
- Being open and heart-centred.
- Inner peace and harmony.
- Loving yourself and others.
- Joy, delight and ecstasy.
- Child-like playfulness.
- Being highly creative and productive.
- Effortless concentration.

- Work feeling like play.
- Following your energy.
- Feeling energised by life.
- Attracting 'good luck'.
- Meaningful coincidences.
- Being in the 'right place at the right time'.
- Clarity of higher purpose.
- Receiving clear inner guidance.
- Trusting your inner wisdom.
- Focusing on what really matters to you.
- Seeing the 'bigger picture' of your life.
- Sense of complete freedom – anything is possible.
- Expanded or mystical awareness.
- Honouring your emotions.
- Being spontaneous and uninhibited.
- Enjoying the 'simple pleasures' of life.
- Solving problems with ease.
- Life feeling easy and effortless.
- Feeling at one with your body.
- Enjoying silence and solitude.
- Natural tendency to balance your life.
- Vibrant health and vitality.
- Sense of timelessness – time might seem to expand, *or* to pass rapidly, but it feels *different* from 'clock time'.
- Living your Dreams.
- Appreciating the wonder of nature.
- Reverence for all life.
- Gratitude.
- Radiating love, light and joy to others.

2

Wild and Free

In short, all good things are wild and free.

HENRY DAVID THOREAU

SOFT TIME IS warm and moist and earthy. It feels like sinking our hands into the wet brown clay of a spinning potter's wheel. It gently reaches deep down into our roots, our core, our very soul. Life becomes an almost unbearably rich experience. Yesterday I walked on a trail alongside a drystone wall covered in mosses and lichens in myriad shades of green. Just gazing at this living wall became a peak experience for me; for a moment, I *was* sun-warmed slabs of stone dressed in soft mosses, snaking across the landscape. (My Hard Time mind would have barely noticed it – categorising it under 'wall', then ignoring it – but, at least for the moment, I was in Soft Time.)

Mythologist Joseph Campbell once said that people were not so much searching for *meaning* in their lives, as for an *experience of aliveness.* When we live in Soft Time, we feel vibrantly alive – and a key to this is reconnecting with our bodies, and with nature, which take us beyond our ego to our deep Self. When we live in Soft Time, we feel embodied right down to the tips of our fingers and toes. *Every* experience connects us more deeply with our soul, our body, our aliveness. Our Soft Time body-mind is vast, connected, timeless, synergistic. It *is* life. It *is* everything. It allows us the kind of wild and earthy spirituality which Hildegarde of Bingen, the remarkable 11th century Rhine mystic, called 'moist and green'.

We need to reclaim our wildness. This does not mean going crazy or losing control. It means reconnecting with our instinctive psyche, our wise and knowing self, our heart-self, that part of us which knows at a gut level what is true, how we feel, what we long for, what we need to do and when – the part of our self which is still connected with the Oneness. Hidden beneath the surface gloss of our 'civilised' ego-self is our wild Self – which dwells naturally in Soft Time.

During the Second World War, the United States had an air-force base in Alaska. At times, the aircraft would develop mechanical problems which flummoxed their engineers – but local Inuit people who had never seen an engine would amble up, smilingly put their hands inside and fix the problem.[1] Like many primitive people who live in harmony with nature, the Inuit were still in touch with their deep Self, who is indivisibly part of All That Is. They were not limited to mere *rational* knowledge – the knowledge of the ego-self, the tip of the iceberg – but could tap into *any* information through the undivided energy field of Nature.

Children, too, often know what they are not 'supposed' to know – until they learn that such things are impossible. Studies of psychic experiences in children have found that telepathy, clairvoyance and precognition peak around the age of four (although psychokinetic abilities such as spoon-bending are strongest between seven and 14 years of age).[2] Research suggests that extrasensory perception is linked with the older, more 'primitive' parts of the brain – the cerebellum and brainstem – which supports the idea that such skills were once normal, and have simply been forgotten. Long before adulthood, most of us have buried our psychic skills in a locked casket labelled *'Impossible – do not open'* – and have learnt to see the 'paranormal' as science-fiction or fairytales.

Yet our wild Self is still there, gently tugging at our sleeves in its own unique way. Our wildness speaks to us through dreams and images, body language, 'gut feelings', memories which rise unbidden, daydreams and fantasies, physical symptoms. In moments of peace and solitude, we might even hear its voice. It is heart-centred and loving – but with a raw edge, a passion, a sensuality, a sense of embodiment, so that it roars rather than purrs. (The passionate and *fierce* love that a mother feels for her baby comes from her Wild Woman.)

As Clarissa Pinkola Estés points out,[3] our wild Self helps to re-establish balanced cycles of work, play, creativity and sexuality – like the rhythms of nature. Without our wildness, we don't know how to pace ourselves. We are too 'nice' and make life-sapping choices, giving away our power to others. When we reclaim our wild Self, we are wise, powerful, creative and intuitive. We are fearlessly individualistic. We are passionate and spontaneous. Our relationships gain new meaning and depth. We live from the heart. Like all good things, we are wild and free.

Within psychology, there is a growing ecopsychology movement[4] which suggests that much of our anxiety, depression and addiction comes not from childhood experiences or personal neurosis, but from feeling over-civilised, over-controlled and alienated from the natural world – which has cut us off from our deep Self, our wild Self. Modern society is literally driving us crazy!

Today, many of us live in grey urban sprawls, with miles of concrete and tarmacadum broken only by diligently mown lawns and isolated trees, with city lights so bright that we can barely see the stars at night. It is hardly surprising if we feel lonely and alienated. Instead of hearing a symphony of birdsong, bubbling streams and rustling leaves each day, we might face a constant roar of traffic, ringing of phones, bells and car alarms, the disembodied sounds of radio or television, and droning of computer screens. We grow pale under artificial lights, then lie on sunbeds to fake a tan. Our homes and offices are carefully insulated to exclude the weather, the seasons, the insects and birds. Many people go for weeks or months without watching the sun rise, or noticing the cycles of the moon. For some of us, the natural world seems to be eliminated from our daily lives, scrubbed out like a dirty mark. It is something we see on our TV screens, sandwiched between commercials for washing powder and deodorants: sanitised and unthreatening.

Our hearts surely long for meadows filled with wild flowers, great old forests, crashing oceans, rushing streams and tranquil lakes – for the wildness and grandeur of the natural world. Our souls are hungry for the earth. Deep down, we 'know' that nature can be a stepping stone into the ancient magic – the mystical, the timeless, the unseen, the deep, the numinous, the sacred. Nature belongs to Soft Time. The Kalahari bushmen have observed that modern people have a great longing 'to walk again with the moon and stars'. We long to feel at one with nature. We yearn to be free like a bird or a river.

Mountains are huge contemplatives. Rivers and streams offer voice; they are the tears of the earth's joy and despair. The earth is full of soul.

JOHN O'DONOHUE[5]

Fear of the wild

Yet we are also *afraid* of the wild. Our Hard Time self – our ego – is tame and over-civilised. It is cool, dry, fast, heady and analytical. It sees the physical body as a mere appendage to our brain. It *observes* life, feeling separate, cut off, contained. For the ego-self, nature is a collection of objects; it is Other. It defines wildness as savage, fierce, out of control. It wants to tame it, control it, even destroy it. For our Hard Time self, wildness is dangerous, threatening, unbounded, unpredictable. Some of us never venture out into the countryside at all, feeling 'safer' in our homes, our gardens, in front of a television. We are scared of our wild Self.

This conflict between our longing for wildness and our fear of it is demonstrated vividly in the Lake District

National Park where I live. It is a once-glacial paradise of lakes, mountains, woods and rolling valleys, which draws around 12 million visitors each year, and offers 18,000 miles of footpaths. Yet according to surveys, the average day-tripping motorist walks *less than 60 metres* – just about far enough to shuffle from their car to a café or gift shop.[6] Apart from a few popular routes, the footpaths are mostly deserted, while the small Lakeland towns and villages are usually heaving with visitors.

A friend who used to lead Outward Bound courses in the mountains admits that she had a series of nightmares when she first ventured on to the fells alone; and many participants in my retreat-workshops in the Lakes have confessed that they felt fearful of losing sight of houses, roads and other man-made landmarks – although they longed to wander alone on the fells. Our deep Self is drawn to the wild, but it terrifies our ego-self.

Perhaps it is essential to 'feel the fear and do it anyway'? If we really want to integrate our wildness, I believe we need to spend time in truly wild places – and preferably alone. ('Alone' comes from 'all-one', meaning whole or integrated.) As Wordsworth put it, 'a wilderness is rich with liberty'. It is deeply healing – and perhaps essential to our mental health – to be in nature. It reconnects us with the divinity of the earth, and our interrelatedness with all beings. It gives us a sense of belonging. It is a soothing balm which helps us slow down and shift into Soft Time.

Gardens, city parks and even farmland are all very well, but they do not carry the healing energy of wilderness. Wilderness feeds and nourishes the soul. Thoreau spent two years in virtual solitude at Walden Pond – and emerged with transcendental wisdom which still affects our hearts and minds today. As he put it, 'I went to the woods because I wished to live deliberately, to front only the essential facts of life, and see if I could not learn what it had to teach, and not, when I came to die, discover that I had not lived.'[7]

Anything which releases our spontaneity, passion and creativity will *help* to reconnect us with our wild Self – such as free dancing, drumming, abstract act, theatre improvisation, singing freely or making love with abandon – but perhaps it is only in the wild, becoming like a wild creature, that we reach the depths of our natural self, our heart, our soul.

Only by going alone in silence, without baggage, can one truly get into the heart of the wilderness. All other travel is mere dust and hotels and baggage and chatter.

JOHN MUIR

A quest for the wild Self

Several years ago, just after dawn in the Colorado Rockies, I set off on a vision quest under the direction of a Huichol shaman. My aim: to reconnect with my wild Self.

I wear jeans and a T-shirt, and carry a light backpack containing a tiny candle, an almost empty box of matches, a quartz crystal, a sweatshirt, a thin square of blanket, and a small piece of chocolate (as an offering to the Earth). No food. No water. No sleeping bag. No watch or clock. I leave camp after a special ceremony at dawn, and make my way across steep meadows and alongside a mountain stream, clamber over rocky crags and walk along forest tracks.

Eventually I feel an inner urge to enter the darkness of the forest – and minutes later, I emerge from the trees near the edge of a ravine, which offers panoramic views over a vast valley and across to high snow-capped peaks many miles away. This is to be my sacred spot.

I gather stones to mark my small circle, placing them according to Huichol tradition, and bury my offering deep in the earth. Then I sit upon my blanket beneath a gnarled old tree, sheltering from the blistering heat of the sun, and offer prayers and chants. I am to sit upon this spot within the sacred circle for the next 24 hours. My throat is already dry.

As I sit, I become aware of our total dependence on the earth. The water that I normally drink without awareness is a gift from the Earth. I trace my usual diet back to its sources in nature, and realise how distant a cheese sandwich or chocolate bar seems from the earth, almost as if such things were made by human beings, conjured out of thin air. I consider all of the everyday items we take for granted – candles, matches, blankets, radios, sofas, videos – and I trace them back to the earth. I feel deep gratitude – and become conscious of how much I take for granted.

As the hours pass, I become acutely aware of the cycles of time. As the sun rotates around me, the shadows grow shorter, creatures hide or become still in the midday sun. I am aware of cycles within cycles: days within the moon cycles, sun cycles within the cycles of the seasons. Time seems to be circular.

Sitting in this sacred circle, hour after hour, I begin to reconnect with the natural woman, the Wild Woman within me. She 'knows' that the birds and trees and rocks are alive and conscious. She listens to the voice of the breeze, and the wisdom of the mountains. She knows that every stone has its song to sing. This Wild Child would only uproot a plant after asking its permission, and only take from the earth what she really needs. She belongs to the earth.

To my surprise, as time passes I do not feel particularly hungry or thirsty. As the sun rises and falls, I feel so much a part of the earth that hunger and thirst seem unnecessary. Everything I need is here. I am at peace. I am safe. A prairie dog comes to the edge of my circle, twitching with curiosity. I silently speak to it, and it returns again and again. A hawk circles overhead. We 'speak' to each other. Everything has a voice. I 'see' the spirit of a native American – a proud, muscular young man – who comes to stand on a huge flat rock in front of me, looking out across the valley. I sense that he is on a hunting trip. I watch him for some time before he gently fades away. All of this seems perfectly natural.

The sun sinks behind the distant mountains, and night closes in. I have always been afraid of the dark. The possibility of a mountain lion or bear nearby does not concern me; it is nothing compared with my fear of the night. My tiny candle soon flickers and burns out, and it is a moonless night. Pitch black. I cannot see my own hands. Panic rises. My heart begins to pound faster and faster. 'What if . . .?' I remind myself to breathe, and let go. I focus on my breathing, releasing the tension. Slowly, breath by breath, I pass through the tunnel of fear . . . . I face the mountain coldness wrapped in my thin blanket, and know I will survive. *Initiation*. And at the first glimmer of the grey light of dawn,

I reach up to the stars with arms that seem to be boundless. Star Woman. Hawk Person. Wild Child. Unafraid of the night.

As the sun rises, I am enraptured by the beauty and magnificence of the landscape. I have never felt so alive. With my heart bursting, I stand to greet the dawn. Night slowly becomes day – and, somewhat reluctantly, I fold my blanket and dismantle the sacred circle. I feel sad at the prospect of returning to civilisation. I want to stay. I have found a missing part of my Self in that mountain wilderness. My soul has descended into my body. I feel as if I have come home.

I begin to walk and suddenly realise that I am badly dehydrated and very weak. I meander back towards base camp, but cannot remember the route. After the clarity of the vision quest, my mind now seems hazy. I realise I should not have walked so far from camp without taking bearings. My Hard Time self takes over. I begin to feel frightened, and my experience of oneness deserts me. I might wander here for days without meeting a human being. Could I survive in the wilderness? According to sacred tradition, I must not drink any water until I return to base camp. Will I collapse and die? My legs weaken and wobble; my tongue is cracked and dry. As the sun rises higher in the sky, I become more and more lost. Afraid, I call out to Spirit for help.

Then I have another vision. I 'see' a spirit Deer appear just in front of me – the power animal of the Huichols. It turns in the opposite direction, and trots ahead of me. I retrace my steps and follow it up a grassy hill and across a stream. Although I know that the deer is from the imaginal realms, it is no more or less real to me than the trees and mountains. The concept of realness no longer makes sense to me. Inner and outer have blended into a seamless fabric. Before long, I recognise a long curving track which leads back to the camp – and the spirit animal vanishes. As I re-enter the camp, my heart is filled with gratitude . . . .

A few months after my vision quest in the Colorado mountains, I radically changed my lifestyle and work patterns to create more space for myself. My Wild Woman was being set free! Reclaiming the wild Self is not an overnight affair – and many years on, I am still learning to wear the pelt of my Wild Woman – but I'm getting there. Slowing down the pace of my life has helped enormously. Living in the heart of the Lakes – and walking, walking, walking – has helped. Becoming a mother has released even more of my natural self. (Is there anything so wild, earthy, beautiful and primal as giving birth?) Yet I feel sure that my Wild Woman has yet to sing her sweetest, or roar her loudest.

Now I see the secret of the making of the best persons.
It is to grow in the open air, and to eat and sleep with the earth.

WALT WHITMAN

Natural ecstasy

In our hi-tech world, many people have lost touch with the 'natural ecstasies'[8] of life: the crimson and purple of a stormy winter sunset, the first snowdrops of spring, the warmth of a summer breeze on the skin, the drifting scent of purple jasmine, rusty falling leaves in an autumn wood-land. Or the sensual joys of wild dancing, eating a ripe plum, making love on cool satin sheets, walking barefoot on the earth or sailing on the ocean. Or the ecstasy of the arts: the bliss of a Mozart symphony, the inspiration of Blake or Yeats, the delight of an impressionist painting. Or the simple joys of friendship, love and companionship.

As we become separated from our wild Self, our natural self, our body-mind, our deep Self, the simple pleasures of life can no longer satisfy us, no longer fill us, no longer heal us. We might walk amidst a beautiful garden, or lie in bed with our lover, or attend a concert, yet somehow we do not feel *present*. We feel like a detached observer – empty, numb, unmoved, untouched. The colours seem drab, the sounds muted, all of our senses dulled. We are so full of thoughts, so much 'in our head', that there is no space to *experience* our lives. Body, mind and soul are split asunder. And we wonder what is wrong with us.

The mystical approach to recovering our aliveness is to reconnect with our body, with our sensuality, with our passion, with our natural Self. I once heard a young woman, still a teenager, on the radio. She had sailed around the coast of Britain single-handed in a small yacht. Had she ever felt lonely on her trip, asked the interviewer? Not at all, she said, sounding surprised. During the months of preparation, she and her boat had become 'good friends' – so once she set sail, she always had her boat for company, as well as the sea and sometimes wild creatures too. 'How could I possibly have felt lonely?' she asked. This is the voice of the embodied mystic, the magical child, the Wild Child within us all. It is our sacred Self – and it is a key to living in Soft Time.

3

In Search of the Holy Grail

The angels keep their ancient places;
Turn but a stone and start a wing!
'Tis ye, 'tis your estranged faces,
That miss the many-splendoured thing.
FRANCIS THOMPSON[1]

THIS AFTERNOON, I wandered down to Rydal Water with my toddler. As we arrived at our favourite shore, a pair of swans glided towards us, hoping for food. I rustled our bag of bread and they closed in, circling and wagging their tails. Ten minutes later, as I handed the last piece of bread to my son, I realised that I had been lost in a stream of thought about my writing – not only while feeding the swans, but all the way down to the lake. I might as well have been at home.

As I become aware of this, giggling at myself, I allow my mind to clear and suddenly – snap! – I am *there* at the lakeside; not just seeing but *experiencing* the graceful arch of those strong white feathered necks, rippling reflections on the water, fragments of soggy bread, a pair of pecking yellow beaks, and my son's shiny little blue wellingtons. I look down at my own hands and feet, amazed at being *in* this wonderful scene, at *belonging* to the world. I am in Soft Time again – and the joy of aliveness sweeps through me . . . .

Since living in Soft Time is paradise on earth, why don't we all *stay* in Soft Time permanently? Why do so many people feel that life is passing them by, that they do not feel fully alive? Why are so many lives either dull and unfulfilling or even hellish and traumatic? How did we lose touch with our wild Self, our deep Self?

The answer to these questions begins with a story. . . . It is a short story about the long evolution of human consciousness – who we are as human beings, where we have come from, and where we are going. (*Warning*: This story might make your Hard Time self feel a little nervous.)

The birth of the ego

Long, long ago – before time as we know it began – human beings were not aware of themselves as separate individuals. Like a shoal of fish who twist and turn simultaneously as if with 'one mind', we had only group consciousness. We were part of the earth, part of nature, part of each other.

Deep in the heart of every human being was a divine Light which shone a brilliant Light-energy into the universe – and all of the Lights formed one Light together. If we needed to know where to find fruit, or where a child had wandered to, or when the weather would favour a journey, we looked in our hearts – and in that moment, we 'knew'. There was no separateness. There was only the one Light. We lived in harmony with each other and with the planet.

Time was circular, and all that changed was the seasons, the movements of the stars, the cycles of birth and death: the rhythms of nature. This eternal, timeless age is remembered in our mythologies as the Garden of Eden.

Then came the first glimmers of our self-awareness, of 'me'-ness. As our consciousness evolved, we began to realise that you-are-not-me: the birth of the ego. We had decided to explore our 'masculine' energy, our individuality, our separateness. Gradually, almost imperceptibly at first, we began to separate ourselves from the oneness of All That Is – from nature, from our Source, from each other, from the Light. This emerging feeling of separateness led to anxiety. The Light in our hearts became clouded by fear, and started to fade from our awareness.

Thousands of years passed, and the ego-self began to take charge. It rose like a dark battleship from the vast ocean of 'feminine' energy, of Oneness. The patriarchal sky-god religions were born – such as Judaism and Christianity – and violently suppressed the earth-based Goddess religions of old. The holy trinity of virgin, mother and crone was replaced by father, son and holy ghost. Her temples were destroyed, and Her festivals replaced by those of the sky-god. God/Goddess – who had once been seen as everywhere and everything – was redefined as masculine, as 'out there', as separate from us.

We began to feel like exiles in a strange and hostile land. Our bodies felt like prisons. Instead of loving Mother Earth – our home – we began to loot, exploit, rape and try to control her. We fought and killed each other. The world was no longer a paradise; it was now seen as unfriendly and unsafe. Life was to be endured rather than enjoyed. Fear came to dominate our lives, and we strived more and more to protect ourselves, to gain control, to make ourselves feel safe. Having lost touch with our inner wisdom, our Light, we turned outside ourselves for guidance, comfort and security – to priests, gurus, 'experts'; we trusted them, and blamed them when they were wrong.

Deep down, we yearned for our lost sense of Oneness, of wholeness, our Light. We had lost our sense of the sacred, our awe and wonder, our joy and delight, our dreams and myths and magic. We had abandoned the spirit world. We felt anxious, lonely and disconnected. We were living in Hard Time.

Then – amidst all the rush and busyness and fear – emerged a few beings who remembered, or even saw the Light. Others treated them as crazy at first – and they were bullied, threatened, even murdered. But there were others who saw the Light too – more and more of them. Some kept quiet for fear of what might happen. Others believed that the Light belonged to one or more 'special' beings, and worshipped *them*. Yet others saw the Light everywhere, and felt it pulsing within their own hearts, urging them to witness the Light as universal – and they began to speak out.

Most beings still dismissed stories of the Light, or were too busy to pay any attention – but more and more hearts began to open, to listen, to dare to hope that it might be true. In the big noisy marketplaces, the Light was still ignored – but in private places, in silence and solitude and stillness, amongst those who listened in the spaces between words, the clouds of fear began to fade, and the eternal Light began to shine through. People began to live from their hearts, to work in co-operation and harmony, and to

hold a vision of heaven-on-earth once again. The Light of a
new golden age began to shine . . . .

Return to the Source

As I understand it, humanity is literally at a turning point in
history – as we begin to spiral back towards our Source.
Our journey has reached its farthest point. We have paid a
heavy price for our exploration of masculine ('yang')
energy. The fear and apparent separateness of the ego are
responsible for almost all of our traumatic history – wars
and battles of every kind, the Crusades and Inquisition,
witch-hunting, the genocide of Jews, Tibetans and native
Americans, the atomic bomb, destruction of the rainforests,
radioactive waste, toxic pollution, the hole in the ozone
layer, our vanishing countryside, rape, child abuse, free-
floating anxiety, depression, addiction and co-dependency
. . . . You name it, and the ego-self can probably be blamed
for it!

However it is not all gloomy news. The ego has at least
given us enough self-awareness to *see* what a mess we have
made! And if we stand back far enough to see the whole
picture, we can take a deep breath and realise that everything has happened according to plan. Long ago, we knew
that separating from the Oneness would create fear, struggle, conflict and darkness – but we trusted that we would
find our way Home again. We always had faith that, as the
mystic Dame Julian of Norwich put it, 'All will be well, and
all will be well, and all manner of things shall be well . . .'.

Having developed our separate ego-self to its limits –
along with language, culture, religion, the arts, science and

technology – we are now beginning to reconnect with the Oneness, to remember who we really are. However, we are not going back. We are not losing our sense of individuality, of uniqueness. On the contrary, we are evolving into a new species of human being whom we might call *homo spiritus* – aware both of our individuality *and* our Oneness.

> *We shall not cease from exploration*
> *And the end of all our exploring*
> *Will be to arrive where we started*
> *And know the place for the first time.*
> T.S. ELIOT[2]

'I think, therefore I am'

So – what exactly is the ego-self, and what do we need to know about it?

Our ego, or conscious self, is what we usually think of as 'I' or 'me'. It is our normal waking consciousness (though Gurdjieff, the mystical teacher, and others would say it is asleep rather than awake). Its centre is in the left hemisphere of the brain – the rational, thinking side – so although it *can* access the right brain, the ego-self prefers to think about and analyse situations. It is comfortable with thoughts, with logic, with 'common sense'. It is good at bluffing, pretending, trying to impress, skimming along on the surface of life. It denies or dismisses mystery, hidden realities, the unknown – in fact, anything that challenges its limited assumptions about the world.

Our ego-self tends to be chronically fearful and insecure. It nervously tries to fill our minds with superficial chitter-chatter to drown out its anxiety, chase away scary emotions and avoid feelings of emptiness. It is afraid of silence and stillness. It is frightened of what might bubble up to awareness: perhaps emotions which threaten to overwhelm it, or intuitions which are 'illogical', or experiences which are too intense. So it fills our awareness with its never-ending stream of chatter instead – or switches on the TV and radio 'for company'.

There is a Calvin and Hobbes cartoon in which Calvin's mother wrenches him away from the TV screen and thrusts him into the garden for some fresh air, amidst his loud protests that the outside world is 'Too hot, too bright, too humid, too buggy . . . too *real!*' It is frighteningly close to the truth. The ego sees life as a battle zone, so it tries to erect safety barriers between itself and the world: a TV screen, a computer monitor, a car windscreen, a professional role, smart clothes or a thick layer of make-up all help make it feel a little safer.

The ego describes, labels, categorises and compares events, rather than *inhabiting* the subtlety, richness and depth of what is happening. 'This is a sunset, and I've seen sunsets before', 'This is breakfast, just like any other morning', says the ego-self, using its constant chitter-chatter to separate itself from the immediacy and uniqueness of experience of our body-mind, or natural self. (It categorises people in the same way, preferring the prejudice of 'us and them' to the rich reality of unique individuals.)

The ego is often *intrigued* by emotion, rather as if feelings come from another planet. It might enjoy the safe, vicarious emotion of soap operas and gossip – but it avoids genuine emotion. The ego-self wants and needs to be in control – so our own emotions are often squashed and tucked away in the older body-mind or subconscious, or merely 'analysed' as curiosities.

It has a nervous need to be busy, so the ego often *creates* problems to keep itself occupied. If it has nothing to think or worry about, it simply invents things. Its awareness spins around in tight little spirals, so it gets obsessed with details and trivia – such as counting calories, worrying about pimples, train-spotting, gossiping about neighbours, re-arranging Tupperware, reading the back of cereal packets, learning what a film star rubs into her skin, or discovering what computer software can do that you will never, ever, need it to do.

Seeing through the eyes of the limited ego is like looking down the wrong end of a telescope. What is 'real' to the ego is only what you can see and hear and touch, what can be proved, what makes rational sense. It is a small world – which copes admirably while peering into computer screens or ticking off checklists, but is like an ostrich trying to fly when it comes to our Dreams and visions, our relationships, our life purpose or spiritual growth.

Our ego-self lives by ulterior motives. Whatever it *seems* to be doing – shopping, working, watching TV, going to church, giving to charity, helping an old lady across the street – you can be sure that the ego has a hidden agenda: to feel safe, to gain power, to control and manipulate, to feel good (often at others' expense), to seek approval, to avoid responsibility, to avoid emotion or intimacy, to avoid change and growth. The ego takes itself very seriously and rarely relaxes; after all, 'It's a jungle out there!'

There is a story about Mahatma Gandhi which beautifully illustrates the fearfulness of the ego. He was summoned to an office of the British Empire in India, and as he entered the room, a line of uniformed British soldiers raised their rifles and held Gandhi in their sights. Gandhi – a small thin man wearing only a homespun robe, who could not pose any physical threat – looked at the soldiers with compassion, and said 'You must be very frightened'.

Finally, the ego-self feels inadequate. Deep down, it knows that it is small and limited – so if we over-identify with our ego, we tend to feel chronically insecure and 'not good enough', or we compensate with delusions of grandeur, arrogance and pomposity. (The ego is at its strongest in late adolescence and early adulthood, when we are leaving home and building our own identity – which is why adolescents can be so selfish, egotistical and arrogant at times! Our ego-self and our 'inner adolescent' are remarkably similar.³)

Our ego is not to be blamed or judged for all its defences, distractions, insecurities and hidden agendas. It feels scared and inadequate *because* it is disconnected from the experience of oneness, from our body, from nature, from our deep Self, from love. *The problem is that we have lost touch with the more 'feminine' aspects of the Self which are essential to living in Soft Time.* The poor ego has been doing its best, but it has been overloaded with tasks which are quite beyond its ability. It feels very small and alone, and is trying to protect itself – like a frightened young child who has lost its mother.

Paradise lost

The metaphor of a lost or abandoned child – split off from the Divine Mother – is very close to reality. When we enter the world, the split-off ego is often symbolically acted out as we are cleaved from our biological mother – thus setting the scene for a future in Hard Time.

For a new-born baby, freshly arrived from a reality of pure love and light, birth is an exciting yet potentially traumatic event. Its moist, warm, dark, nourishing mother-womb-heartbeat has been its sanctuary in physical reality until now. There has been no inside *and* outside, no mother *and* self – just the experience of oneness.

Then the baby is thrust inexorably into a strange new world. As it emerges, it desperately needs reassurance that it has not been ripped asunder from the oneness. It needs love, warmth, tenderness, gentle light and its mother's already-familiar voice. It needs the reassurance of skin-to-skin contact with its mother's soft belly and breasts. It needs an atmosphere of unhurried calm and welcome – *a sacred space* – so that it can emerge into this new experience with a feeling of safety and trust: 'The world is a safe and loving place to be'. If these basic needs are met, the baby is born calm, quiet, serene, curious and *very* alert. (I saw this for myself when my son was born at home two years ago, in what was – for me – a drug-free, pain-free and ecstatic experience.)

All too often, a new-born baby has a very different start to life. It is met by brutal lights, harsh and unfamiliar voices, rushing and anxiety, wires and monitors, surgical gloves, forceps and strong antiseptic smells. It might be drugged from its mother's 'pain relief', have sensors attached to its tender scalp, and panic as it struggles to breathe due to the premature cutting of its pulsating, oxygen-giving cord. After a brief cuddle, it is swept away from its mother to be weighed on hard metal scales, checked over, washed and swaddled. It might be offered a cold rubber teat and bottle rather than its mother's soft, warm, cuddly breast and familiar heartbeat. And soon enough, it is put in a motionless cot (or even an incubator) – all alone – to sleep. It is a birth which only our ego-self could design. Such a baby faces separation, helplessness, terror, abandonment and even assault. *Welcome to the world, little one!* No wonder it screams! No wonder it seems to be in a blank state of shock, or retreats quickly into sleep!

Medicalised childbirth pays little heed to the exquisitely sensitive and vulnerable *psyche* of the new-born baby, or the (often deeply buried) instincts of the mother, both of which are screaming out for love and unbroken oneness. Attitudes to childbirth have certainly shifted since the 'dark ages' of medical hegemony in the 1970s – thanks to pioneers such as Frederick Leboyer and Michel Odent; but how much has *really* changed? Hospital birth is still the norm; drugs and other medical intervention are still seen as routine; some mothers still (bizarrely) give birth lying on their backs; and the predominant mood is so often anxiety and urgency. Less than one in four babies is fully breastfed for even six weeks; and babies fresh from the womb are *still* left to sleep in a lonely cot – even if it is now at the mother's bedside.

If young animals are separated from their mother shortly after birth, even for a short time, we know that the psychic damage can be severe and permanent – but for human babies, separation has become the norm. All too often, a baby is treated as a commodity to be slipped into the busy timetable of a Hard Time lifestyle. The baby spends much of its day imprisoned in a playpen, bouncy chair or pram, and is expected to sleep on its own – without the physical touch it constantly craves and needs. After a few weeks or months, the mother often returns to work, leaving her infant with a nursery or a series of childminders, as if all that a baby needs is feeding, nappy-changing, sleep and play. *Its primary emotional need for secure bonding and physical contact is almost ignored.* (A baby lives in the eternal 'now'; it cannot know that mother will reappear after a few hours; it only knows that she is *not here*, that a crucial part of its own wholeness is *not here*.)

We see it as 'normal' for babies to cry – often for two or more hours every day – but a baby's cry is a last resort, an emergency distress call for reunion with its mother/caretaker. We see it as 'normal' if a young child sucks its thumb or needs a blanket, dummy, teddy bear or other transitional object in order to go to sleep – rather than a warning sign that the child's basic needs are perhaps not being met, that it is suffering from separation anxiety, that it feels unsafe in the world. Babies do not need fluffy teddy bears, 'womb music', rocking cradles or brightly-coloured mobiles to entertain them in their abandoned solitude; they need the warm touch and unconditional love of a real live person.

In 'first-world' cultures, a mother generally keeps her baby close to her body for many months after birth – day *and* night – while she carries on with her routine as usual, until the *baby* initiates separation from the mother by starting to crawl. Then she remains within easy reach of her wandering and exploring infant, still nursing on demand for two to four years, and giving help only when required. (Their babies almost never cry; and their children seem to grow up joyful and self-reliant, and rarely argue or fight.) Psychotherapist Jean Liedloff – who spent two years living with the Yequana indians in South America – suggests that the infant who is held 'in arms' is in a state of bliss, while an infant out of arms is in 'a state of longing in the bleakness of an empty universe'.[4]

For a woman, pregnancy, childbirth and early mother-hood can and should be a mystical experience – a blissful time of merging into oneness, breaking down the bound-aries of 'I-and-not-I', as we merge with our baby's growing body-mind and are no longer 'alone' in the world. (There is no equivalent to pregnancy for men, though many perhaps seek this sense of union through sex.) A biological mother is supposed to be a connecting thread to the Great Mother, the feminine face of God, mystical union, the Oneness – and her natural Self 'includes' her baby for a long time after birth (perhaps forever).

I had a memorable reminder of this merging when my son was five months old, and I went to the hairdresser for the first time since his birth. He was close at hand with his father, but it felt strange to be doing something 'for me'. I had never been separated from my baby – carrying him everywhere in a sling, nursing him on demand, sharing a bed with him. While my hairdresser firmly massaged shampoo into my scalp, I thought anxiously to myself, 'She is pressing quite hard – *I hope she knows about the fontanelles*' (the soft spot on a baby's scalp). Moments later, I realised that my head was *not* my baby's head – and was intrigued to find that my boundaries firmly included my son, that he felt so much part of me that 'my head' and 'his head' could easily be confused.

As I see it, early separation of mother and child – along with all that this entails, such as being cut off from our deep Self – makes it unlikely that a baby's basic needs will be met. As a child we often cope with the situation by fragmenting – by sacrificing our wholeness and integrity, burying our love, light and wisdom somewhere deep inside, and developing our superficial ego-self to deal with the world. This allows two destructive core beliefs to take root and flourish:

1. *'The world is a dangerous place to be.'* (FEAR)
2. *'I am not good enough' (or 'I am unloved').* (SHAME)

Either of these assumptions would make life pretty miserable. Together, fear and shame guarantee living in Hard Time. The ego-self becomes fixated at the level of the child or adolescent, and is unable to mature – and life becomes a constant struggle to feel safe and secure, and/or to feel 'good enough'. Is this how we – and our children – have been programmed to spend our lives? It is certainly what many psychotherapists devote their working lives to healing.

(Of course, babies do differ – and *some* babies emerge from the womb as little Buddhas who are smiling and serene whatever happens, while other babies need constant physical contact and reassurance, due to their own or their mother's psychology, or both. A mother's *attitude* to separation can also make a big difference. If a mother/caretaker is a natural mystic and returns to work, say, feeling connected to her baby and sending calm, loving thoughts – knowing that her baby has been left in loving hands – her baby will experience Oneness without her physical presence. Far more commonly, a mother feels tired, stressed and guilt-ridden, and either 'shuts out' or worries about her baby while she is away – and so transmits separation anxiety to her child.)

It is surely no coincidence that the most aggressive cultures in the world – such as America, Britain and Russia – are those which separate mother and child at birth, wean babies early and expect them to sleep alone in a cot.[5] Our society mirrors its suppression of the feminine, our loss of the divine Mother, by depriving infants of the blissful experience of Oneness with their flesh-and-blood mother/ caretaker that they expect and need in the early months. I see this as one source of the insecure and frightened ego which we see as 'normal'. (There is no blame attached to this; it is simply how parents are *expected* to behave in our culture. Sadly, most first-world cultures are now following in our 'advanced' footsteps and copying our unnatural methods of childbirth and childcare.)

Our mixed approaches to childbirth faithfully mirror our patriarchal society *and* the growing upsurge of the divine feminine. Our anxious ego-self argues that birth is a dangerous and pathological event, which necessitates medical intervention and 'taking control' of the birth process; while our deep Self sees birth as a natural, sacred and mystical experience, urging us to honour the wisdom of the mother's body and the psychic needs of mother-and-baby – to honour the 'feminine' in this most 'feminine' of life's

events. Occasionally, there is a place for medical intervention in childbirth – but like the ego, it has arrogantly taken
control in a situation where our deep Self, our intuitive
body-knowing, is far more appropriate.

Personally I doubt whether good childbirth practice, on
its own, will magically transform the next generation – but
it is a good starting point in recovering our lost Mother. If
birth became a truly sacred experience for mother and
baby, *and* we fulfilled their need for oneness in the months
after birth (perhaps returning to work with the baby
strapped to one's chest), *and* we remained in touch with our
own deep Selves while parenting, might *this* be enough for
our children to grow up without the psychic wounds of fear
and shame that we regard as 'normal' – to have open hearts
and minds, to stay in touch with their inner wisdom, to be
truly 'embodied spirits'? And by parenting in a way that
honours our own deep Self, our intuitive knowing, might
we heal our own childhood wounds in the process? Could
this be the future of humanity, as we return towards the
Source?

True spiritual adulthood

It isn't too surprising that the ego has had a thoroughly bad
press. Spiritual seekers are often urged to beat it up, deny
it, denigrate it, battle with it, even half-kill themselves to
escape its clutches. However, I believe we have to take a
positive and loving approach to the ego. The ego is sick,
wounded and immature – and only love can heal it. If love is
the force that holds everything together – the Grand
Unified Force – then fear is the force that splits us apart,

that divides us against ourselves and each other. If we see *any* aspect of the self as 'the enemy', we are rejecting part of the self – just as the ego has done – which sets up an inner conflict or neurosis. Whatever we resist persists, so it just makes the problem worse.

As we reclaim our divine feminine energy, we must take care to honour our 'divine masculine' too. Our job is to *befriend* our ego-self. The ego was never supposed to be our enemy. It was intended to be a precious gift – the gift of rational thought, of purposeful action, of individuality. (Without the ego, we would either be puppets of our animal instincts, or psychotic and unable to function in the world.) However, it was not meant to take charge of our lives. The problem is that – for the time being – the ego-self not only *runs* the whole show, it believes it *is* the whole show! Overshadowed by fear, the ego has gradually come to dominate our lives – which is why we are having such a Hard Time.

We have come a long way. Over many thousands of years, humanity has evolved through its childhood in the Garden of Eden, then its long period of fearful adolescence in which we developed our ego-self. In the 21st century, I believe we are moving at last into true spiritual adulthood, in which our ego comes into balance with our deep Self, becoming our servant rather than our master. Our ego-self has searched busily and voraciously for happiness and fulfilment outside the Self. The only place it has *failed* to look for the Holy Grail (the chalice, the divine feminine) is where it can be found – deep within our own hearts. The ego has fragmented the Self, leaving us divided against ourselves, but we are now reclaiming our lost wholeness. Our deep mystical Self is, at last, coming Home.

4

The Mystic Heart

The mystic lies deep in every person.
MATTHEW FOX[1]

NEARLY TWENTY YEARS ago, I had a vivid and memorable dream about Hard Time and Soft Time. In the dream, I am in a grey, crowded and noisy factory. Like everyone else, I am playing some kind of board game. The aims and rules of the game are a mystery to me – yet most people are concentrating fervently in small groups, or rushing between boards as if they know exactly what they are doing. I feel too embarrassed to ask anyone what the aim and rules of the game are. Feeling anxious and bewildered, I glance up and notice that the ceiling is made of glass. On the roof sits a beautiful ethereal woman in a long robe of pastel pinks, blues and yellows, with golden tresses of hair tumbling around her. In her left hand, she holds a heart-shaped mirror. She looks down at me, radiant with love – and points at the mirror slowly and meaningfully with a long, elegant finger. Her finger tenderly caresses the shape of the heart, tracing its edge. Her lips are moving, and I strain to hear her above the hubbub around me. Her words are drowned out – yet I am filled with hope and optimism. I ache with longing to reach up to this woman, feeling sure that she represents not only *my* future, but the future of humanity. (It is what native Americans would call a Big Dream.) Then I wake up . . . .

Earth and sky mysticism

> *Do you have a body? Don't sit on the porch!*
> *Go out and walk in the rain!*
>
> KABIR 6:32[2]

What is mysticism? It is ineffable, so cannot be defined in simple terms. Circling around it with words feels like trying to pin down a cloud. It lies beyond language, and is more boundless than the words themselves. It is perhaps easier to say what it includes, or what it might involve. Firstly it is based on direct experience, not rational knowledge – and on *trusting* that experience. It involves knowing and *experiencing* everything as One, while also being aware of one's own individuality – as if a veil has lifted, and the true reality is seen for the first time. It is the 'unthought knowing' which transcends the dualism of mind and body, human and nature, heaven and earth, living and non-living, sacred and secular, good and evil, dark and light, inner and outer, subject and object.

True mysticism is heart-centred, passionate, playful,

open, questioning. It is spontaneous, surprising, unexpected. It celebrates nature and beauty, and is filled with awe. It thrives on silence and solitude. It is the mysterious, the deep, the hidden. It is loving, compassionate and radiant. It is deeply and necessarily creative. And it knows that only love is real – that fear and separateness are illusions. (For our mystic Self, even death holds no fear, since the universe is 'known' to be safe. Death is merely a step into the next great adventure.)

For many years, I believed that mysticism was more or less the same the world over, and throughout the ages. Eventually I realised that there are two kinds of mysticism, which I call natural or earth mysticism and disembodied or sky mysticism.

Disembodied mysticism is based upon denying and denigrating the body, the senses and the earth. It is a false mysticism based on dualism of mind/body and spirit/matter. It aims to 'transcend' the world and invariably involves severe discomfort, terrible pain or even near-death experiences, or (at best) avoiding sensory pleasures. It is a path of growth through struggle – the path of the warrior. The patriarchal world religions such as Hinduism, Buddhism, Judaism and Christianity, as well as some forms of shamanism – the world's oldest religion – tend towards this 'macho' approach to mysticism, which honours only *part* of our feminine energy. (There are, of course, many honourable exceptions such as Francis of Assisi, Hildegarde of Bingen, Meister Eckhart, Julian of Norwich, Mechtild of Magdeburg and – despite his martyred death – perhaps the ultimate example of a natural mystic, Jesus Christ.)

I experienced disembodied mysticism myself when I was anorexic as a young undergraduate. Anorexia is a misguided search for control, self-acceptance and 'perfection' based upon a mind-body split, and conflicts over our feminine energy. (One of my anorexic clients said she felt 'like a nun or monk, starving in piety' — and there is strong link between anorexia and the religious quest.) It involves desperately painful asceticism and self-denial in pursuit of a 'greater ideal' — and is therefore a kind of false mysticism. It certainly didn't bring me enlightenment! As Meister Eckhart pointed out, asceticism merely boosts the ego.

We should be wary of spiritual traditions which define *anything* as less than sacred — the body, sex, money, the earth, the ego, desire — since these encourage us to hate or deny parts of the Self, to push them into our Shadow. Such faiths are dualistic; they are not embracing the divine feminine, the oneness. At a mystical level, there is not — there cannot be — anything which is not God/Goddess.

Natural mysticism is what I see as true mysticism. It is sensual and sensuous, passionate and creative, earth-centred and joyful, wild and free. Whereas the sky mystic strives to *seek* God, the embodied mystic knows that we *are already* God: that 'God is in all things and all things are in God';[3] thus the earth, the body, passion, sexuality and sensuality are all known to be sacred and divine.

The world religion which best honours the divine feminine, in my view, is Taoism. Although Taoism emphasises the need for *balance* of masculine and feminine energy, the *Tao Te Ching* makes it clear that mystical awareness, in its highest form, comes through the feminine spirit, 'the valley spirit', the Mother of all things. It honours all creation, and speaks of the natural joy, spontaneity, freedom, simplicity and power of one who has learnt to live in harmony with the Tao, in tune with the Great Mystery. In a lovely recent translation of the *Tao Te Ching*, it states:

> *Every living thing*
> *Comes from the Mother of Us All:*
> *If we can understand the Mother*
> *Then we can understand her children;*
> *And if we know ourselves as children*
> *We can see the source is Her.*[4]
>
> TAO TE CHING

The spirit of Aloha

Many 'first-world' cultures have taught us about natural mysticism – from the Kogi of Colombia and Australian Aborigines to the Inuits and native Americans – emphasising the divinity of all things, and our need to live in harmony with the earth. The Huna tradition is a wonderful example of natural mysticism, which might have been the original source of Taoism (as well as the wisdom of the Maoris, pygmies, Kalahari bushmen and others). Some say that the Huna wisdom was star-seeded to our planet by extraterres-trials, many thousands of years ago, probably in the region of Tibet – and that it is the oldest and greatest of our mystery schools.

Seven years ago, I read several books about Huna, fell in love with it – and promptly flew to Kaua'i at two days' notice to train with a Hawaiian kahuna.[5] I had studied native American shamanism for years – but this felt different to me, a more 'feminine' form of shamanism. (Serge Kahili King[6] calls it an adventurer approach – based on love, joy and *befriending* our 'enemies' – as distinct from the warrior tradition, which builds strength and wisdom through overcoming adversity.)

In Hawaii, before Christian missionaries invaded their islands, everyone was a natural mystic. The spirit of Aloha is the spirit of unconditional love, and children were taught that 'Aloha is being a part of all, and all being a part of me'.[7] Like the Celts and other earth-centred peoples, the Hawaiians had 'many gods' since they found divinity everywhere. Every tree and stone and creature was sacred and alive. Life was seen as a river which flowed through many lifetimes on earth, allowing us to learn and grow through many different selves – and everyone was seen as responsible for what they created in life. They were connected with their deep Self, and psychic skills were part of everyday life. 'In those days, it was commonplace for people to lie down, and their mind to go elsewhere – to check out weather conditions, to see a loved one far away, to fly with the birds – or to find out the answer to a problem too hard for the mind in body.'[8] They moved giant boulders by asking the stones to become feather-light, called each other home using telepathy, and saw with their 'inner eye'.

The Hawaiians were converted to Christianity – under pressure – because Jesus taught love. However a stark contrast emerged between the Hawaiian and Christian approaches: 'They tried hard. They spoke love, they taught love, but they didn't *know* love. They taught *thou shalt not* – and they were angry with us all the time for having fun and for the laughter and joy in our lives. They were not allowed joy. Salvation came to them only through misery. The Hawaiian gods were far more kind, for they loved happiness and joy as much as they loved sun and rain. They loved bodies the way they were made, glistening with sweat or with water from the ocean. They saw what we were, and it was good.'[9] This is embodied mysticism.

After Christianity came, everything changed in Hawaii. People gradually learnt to see themselves as sinful, and their bodies as shameful. They became materialistic and ambitious. They lost the spirit of Aloha – and there was 'no song in the land'.

The myth of the Fall

Religion has a vested interest in suppressing mysticism, and encouraging us to turn to its own priests and gurus for guidance, rather than seek direct communion with the Divine. After all, mystics are always heretics. They are highly threatening to the ego-self – and therefore to most established religions – since they trust their inner experience, follow their hearts and seek truth rather than dogma. Any religion must protect itself in order to survive as a 'separate' tradition. It has to shut its ears and eyes to more all-encompassing realities. It must cling to the notion of 'us and them' – which can find no home in a mystic heart.

I once heard Paul Solomon say that, while on missionary work in Africa as a Baptist minister, he was amazed when he came to realise that not everyone who was enlightened was a Baptist (or even a Christian)! This would be even more comical if it were not so tragic.

The sky-god religions encourage fall/redemption

theology – that is, the idea that there is something 'wrong' with us that needs to be fixed. Spirit is up-there-and-good, and we are down-here-and-bad. This is an excellent way of controlling and disempowering people! If you feel like a 'miserable earthworm', you will tend to trust in dogma and look up to those in authority – and you will strive hard to be 'good', to gain approval and conform to social norms. This will effectively block your mystic Self. (The Fall is an idea with a germ of truth, since the separation of the ego was a Fall from oneness, and the divine plan is to return Home eventually; thus almost every culture has a mythology of the Fall. However, religion converted this positive and courageous choice of humanity into a 'fall from grace' which needed redemption, to serve its own political agenda.)

Fall/redemption theology gave us the novel concept that the sole purpose of life is *to get somewhere else* – to make it through the pearly gates, to escape the wheel of karma, to pass through the vale of tears, to transcend the body, to seek redemption through martyrhood and suffering. Even in our secular culture, the religious notion of the Fall has permeated our way of life. Workaholism and other widespread addictions are strongly linked with the search for redemption – for feeling good enough, for feeling safe in the world. The 'god' we worship might now be money, success, possessions, duty, status, power, admiration, thinness or beauty – but the process is the same. We feel uneasy about who we are, and how life is, and we are trying to fix it. (Similarly people often feel guilty for so-called indulgences such as eating creamcakes, taking a long holiday or simply doing nothing.) The message is clear: Life is meant to be tough, and we are *not* here to enjoy ourselves! We are 'supposed' to live in Hard Time.

To the earth-centred traditions, this is a bizarre notion. The natural mystic understands that life is an extraordinary divine gift, and that the primary purpose of life is *to live* – to enjoy this wondrous adventure, to revel in the beauty and joy of the earth, to fully inhabit our physical body, to love ourselves and each other. In this view, the earth is not a penal colony for wayward souls; it is a playground, an infinite source of wonder and delight.

The mystical poet Rilke said, 'Being here is so much'. It is such a rich and redolent phrase. *Being here is so much.* It conjures up the warm velvety repose of Soft Time, as well as its immense awe and gratitude. As John O'Donohue puts it, 'It is a strange and magical fact to be here, walking around in a body, to have a whole world within you and a world at your fingertips outside you. . . . It is uncanny how social reality can deaden and numb us so that the mystical wonder of our lives goes totally unnoticed. We are here. We are wildly and dangerously free'.[10]

The divine fire

Yet there is also work to be done. The natural mystic is a practical mystic. When we are fully embodied, we are not passive or indifferent in the face of suffering. We are not aloof from the world, or isolated in a hermit's cell. We *belong* to the world, acknowledging the ego-self which has created so much social and ecological damage – and we want to make a difference. We are passionate and visionary. The true mystic is a balance of divine feminine and divine masculine energy – of higher vision and inspired action – knowing that life is not simply about 'being', it is also about 'becoming'. This means engaging actively with 'what is' and envisioning 'what might be' – then *acting* upon those visions.

As a natural mystic, we trust that everything is unfolding perfectly; *and* we know that we have a small but essential contribution to make to that unfolding. We commit ourselves to being fully alive, fully present, to treading on the face of the earth *and leaving our footprints*.

For me, writing this book is an experience of pure bliss. I wake up filled with eager anticipation, wondering what will unfold on to the blank pages today. My work is my play. I scribble phrases on notepads in the midst of scrubbing pans or tidying toys. I toss ideas around while nursing my son, or discuss them over the dinner table with my husband. Fragments of poems and half-remembered quotes visit me in the bath. Despite having little free time – I care full-time for a toddler who needs little sleep – the book is emerging of its own accord, ahead of schedule. I adore the playful, giggling, hugging, singing, dancing, messing, exploring, merging, contented days spent with my son – and each time he closes his eyes and drifts off to sleep, or my husband takes him off to play, I feel a surge of excitement: it is time to write!

When service comes from the heart, there is no conflict or contradiction between loving our lives and doing our work. For the natural mystic, service is not based upon duty, guilt, obligation or martyrhood. It is part of who we are, of how we freely choose to spend our days. It is part of our balanced cycle of Soft Time and Flow Time – and it feels natural and effortless.

Mysticism and creativity go hand-in-hand. In Bali, the same word means 'human' and 'artist'. As Matthew Fox puts it,

'Every mystic is an artist, and every true artist is a mystic'.[11] When we are fully connected with our deep Self, with Source, with the oneness, whatever we create has a flowing life of its own. Michelangelo spoke of releasing the angel from the uncarved stone in which it was trapped. We become a midwife for the creative expression of our deep Self.

The mystic heart burns with divine fire. A poem tumbles on to the page, every word dazzling in its perfection and astonishment. A painting appears on the canvas which amazes and delights the artist. The creativity of our mystic Self feels effortless, playful, joyful, exhilarating – and totally absorbing. Hours pass like minutes. Mealtimes are ignored. There is a feeling of utter calmness and trust. And finally – yes, this is it! *This* is what needed to be born.

Creativity is not merely a pleasant way to idle away our leisure hours, as our ego-self would have it; nor is it an activity reserved for 'special' or talented people. Creativity is at the core of the mystic way of life. It is about giving birth to our deep Self, about connecting, about paradox, about healing, about transformation. Our mystic Self longs to create – through poetry, dancing, cooking, writing, gardening, sculpting, designing, conversing, making music, or any which way. It knows that nothing comes into existence unless it is first imagined – and that the imagination is the voice of our soul; or, as Barry Lopez puts it, 'it is the imagination that gives shape to the universe'.[12]

The looking-glass world

Mystics have always said that there is no distinction between inner and outer, subject and object – that there is no objective solid reality, despite our scientists' earnest belief that they are discovering more and more about the world 'out there'. The world of separate objects is 'maya', illusion, the false reality of our ego-self, which hides the deeper reality, the oneness of All That Is. According to mysticism, consciousness is the basic building block of the universe – or, as Jung put it, mind and matter are two aspects of one and the same thing. *There is only consciousness*; thus, everything is conscious. There are no objects, only subjects.

If this sounds like mystical mumbo-jumbo to you, remember that many physicists are coming to the same conclusions. Quantum mechanics has tossed into the air some strange paradoxes – such as objects being in two places at once, time running backwards, 'telepathy' between distant particles and a cat that is both-alive-and-dead. Such paradoxes are not a conundrum for our deep Self, which smiles and nods knowingly – but they send classical physicists into a tail-spin!

At the quantum level, everything is interconnected. There are no separate objects, or even solid particles – just a massive web of interrelated energy fields. Some physicists are speculating about an interconnecting holographic field (or 'holofield') – beyond space, time, matter and energy – which connects everything to everything else. Many also suggest that mind and matter do seem to be two sides of the same coin, arising out of the same deeper level of reality – the 'implicate order', quantum vacuum or 'cosmic womb' – which still interacts with everything it has given birth to, and which connects our mind to the rest of the universe.[13]

According to the new physics, *consciousness* is the active agent which collapses the wave of a 'quantum object', thus deciding what is and what is not. Amit Goswami, a professor of physics, goes one step further, saying that if we assume that *consciousness creates the material world* – as mystics have suggested – then 'all the famous paradoxes of quantum physics vanish like the morning mist'.[14] The creative consciousness that he is talking about is not a vast collection of human ego-selves, but the unitive consciousness of All That Is, of which we are an indivisible part.

Let us take another leap of imagination . . . . The mystic within us knows that the world is a mirror. It states in the Upanishads, 'What is within us is also without. What is without us is also within'. Meister Eckhart wrote, 'The world is our soul'. According to the mystical Law of Resonance, like attracts like – so we get what we focus upon. Thoughts are creative energy which we send out into the universe, which then boomerang back to us as people, events and circumstances. In other words, 'thoughts are prayers'. Our beliefs, thoughts, desires, feelings and attitudes attract certain kinds of event, and make other events less likely. Every aspect of life – our home, our work, our family, our friends, our health, our prosperity, our leisure time, how we see the world at large – is a creative act, a reflection of our inner Self. If your home is filthy, cramped and cluttered – or spacious, clean and elegant – it reveals a great deal about your beliefs, personal identity and feelings of worthiness. If your friends are close, loving and supportive (or otherwise), it mirrors how you care for yourself. As we examine our lives, we are gazing into a mirror.

At a practical, down-to-earth level, this mystical insight transforms how we see everyday life. It means there is no luck, no chance, no coincidence. There are no helpless victims – *at a soul level*. We create our own reality.

This gives us tremendous freedom – and total responsibility. We cannot blame our childhood, or the government, or fate, or God, or our boss, or our partner, or anyone else for what happens in our lives; nor can we whinge and complain about what we see happening in the world 'out there'. The buck stops here! (There is no blame or praise attached to this. Our deep Self makes no judgements about what we, or anyone else, choose to create. Every 'problem' is an attempted solution. Every event is an opportunity.)

If the world is a mirror, Hard Time and Soft Time are both self-fulfilling prophecies. Like attracts like. If you believe that life is meant to be a struggle, or that you are undeserving or 'not good enough', then your creative consciousness attracts events, people and situations which reflect your Hard Time beliefs. If you believe, on the other hand, that life is a precious gift, that the universe is loving and supportive, and that you are a loving creative spark of the Divine, then your life will mirror back those core beliefs. This is the astounding nature of our physical reality.

The mystic heart knows that we are not isolated captives in a hard, unfeeling clockwork universe – rather, that we are fellow dancers in a miraculous cosmic starburst of love and imagination. *There is nothing but consciousness.* We have to feel, to experience this truth – to let it seep into our bones, congregate in our cells, simmer in our heart. It is a stunning, breathtaking realisation. God/dess, All That Is, Spirit, the Source, the Force, the Divine, the Beloved – or whatever term you like to use – created us *out of God*, out of Her own body, out of divine consciousness. We co-created ourselves! We are divine sparks of one consciousness – as is everything.

> *Every grain of dust has a wonderful soul.*
>
> JOAN MIRÓ[15]

Whatever we see and experience in the world – from a lemon to a lizard, from a candle to a computer – is simply the light of divine consciousness, trapped light which whizzes around in closed spirals and vibrates at different frequencies. (This book you are holding now *has its own consciousness*. It must have, or it couldn't exist! This is mind-blowing stuff!) As we really begin to take this in – rather than dismissing it as a fairy tale – it helps us transcend all of the dualities which lead us into the prison of Hard Time. It allows us to see everyone and everything as sacred and divine – which, according to the Bhagavad Gita, is a way of leap-frogging into enlightenment.

The old and new physics are powerful metaphors for surface reality and deep reality, for Hard Time and Soft Time. When we live in Soft Time, we inhabit the world of quantum reality. Everything is flowing, harmonious and interconnected. Life feels rich and deep and fascinating. Our consciousness is fluid and mobile. Time expands and becomes our friend. 'Miracles' can happen, and we are showered with meaningful coincidences (what Jung called synchronicities) which confirm that we are living in deep reality – where everything is connected, everything is one, everything is divine love.

The coming age of mysticism

I can see the world's shadow
Becoming a rainbow — and I am
Holding this small globe between my hands
And there is light heat coming
Out from the centre of my palms
God, and my tears are shining . . .

JAY RAMSAY[16]

What of my dream-woman on the glass roof? I saw her as a reminder of the futile busyness of our immature ego, the higher vision of our 'feminine' energy, and the challenge of hearing the voice of our soul above the ego's chitter-chatter. The ego-self is blind to realities beyond space-time, forever restricted by a 'glass ceiling' which seems to separate us from the Divine — but if we stop and pay attention, our deep Self is always there, softly whispering our name. The heart-shaped mirror is symbolic of the mystic heart within each of us — which 'knows' that the world is a mirror, and that love is all that is really real.

As we begin the 21st century, I believe that the feeling of hope my dream-woman gave me is, at last, becoming a reality — that we are shifting inexorably from a *materialist* world view, which imprisoned us in Hard Time, to a *mystical* world view which offers the gift of Soft Time.

There is a lovely Celtic saying, 'The land of eternal youth is behind the house' (*tá tír na n-óg ar chul an ti*).[17] In dream symbolism, a house is the personality — so the saying reminds us that the eternal, the timeless, the mystic Self, the realm of Soft Time, lies hidden just behind our normal everyday self. Heaven is available here and now. We simply have to get out of our own way.

Until recently, only chosen apprentices and spiritual initiates had access to mystical wisdom and practices. Such ideas were considered too sophisticated for the general public, and open to abuse. However, the Hawaiian kahuna – in common with spiritual elders from many other tribes and cultures – long foretold of an age when all the secrets would be told, when the ancient wisdom would become public, and the world would be transformed. We are immensely privileged to live in that age.

Our deep Self is now urging us to follow our heart, to dream the impossible dream, to live with joy and passion, to become a natural mystic. As more and more people awaken to their souls all over the world, and begin to live in Soft Time, it becomes easier and easier to follow in their footsteps. And when we *do* respond to the call of our deep Self – singing our own heart-song, becoming wild and free – I believe that our soul dances and whirls ecstatically, in divine celebration.

PART TWO

1

The Inner Self

1 · FOLLOW YOUR DREAMS

EVERY CHILD KNOWS that life is full of magic – from unicorns and fairy godmothers to angels and Santa Claus. When we are young, we believe that anything is possible, if only we wish for it hard enough and believe in it enough. A child gazes in wonder at a rainbow or a snowflake – and *knows* that miracles happen.

As we grow up, our Hard Time society 'teaches' us that fairies are just make-believe, that it is childish to believe in miracles, that grown-ups know all there is to know, that we mustn't be so foolish and gullible – and we learn to put aside our magical selves, and let go of our Dreams. Bit by bit, the world of magic fades away, until all that is left is a misty memory which occasionally draws a nostalgic sigh from a tired and harassed adult. 'If only such things were real . . .'.

The truth is that the magical world of Soft Time *is* real, and lies just a hair's breadth from us. It might take only a gentle whisper, a silent moment of stillness, a gasp of awe or a heart-felt hug to make the shift. In the pure bliss of Soft Time, we remember that children were right all along: that dreams can and do come true, that miracles happen every day, that the air is filled with sparkle and stardust – for those who are willing to see.

One of the secrets of living in Soft Time is to follow your Dreams – to believe that life is meant to be truly magical, and we are meant to grow through joy. Every spiritual tradition suggests that we are here to learn and grow, but most fail to mention that there are two ways of doing so. We can either face problems and suffering, and hope that overcoming adversity leads us to grow (the Hard Time approach). Or we can grow through the challenges of *learning how to make our Dreams come true*. In other words, we can grow through love, joy and reconnecting with our deep Self (the Soft Time approach).

The word 'enthusiasm' comes from 'en theos', meaning the God within us; in other words, it is a form of higher guidance. Joseph Campbell urged us to 'follow our bliss' – to do what we love, to follow our energy. Passion, joy and enthusiasm lead us towards our higher purpose. If we follow our bliss, we are living in harmony with our deep Self.

Following our Dreams is not about trying to 'have it all' in a driven, compulsive way; nor is it about living for the future, longing for the time when your Dreams have come true, telling yourself 'I'll be happy when . . .'. (That is the path of addiction.) Getting there is not the point. Enjoying the *journey* is what matters.

It is not always an easy path. In the short-term, it is easier to conform, to fit in, to meet the demands of others, to settle for what is expected of you, to allow your Dreams to gather dust. It is always more challenging to follow your heart, to trust your intuition, to believe in your Dreams. After all, it is 'the path less travelled by'. But in the end, it is the only path that is truly joyful and fulfilling.

It is Christmas Eve as I write and – with perfect timing –

the first snow has fallen. The tree is brightly lit and garlanded, with ribboned gifts beneath it. Mince pies and sherry lie on the hearth. There is a sense of joyful anticipation and universal love. There is magic in the air. *Every* day should be like this – and so it can be.

I believe in my Dreams. I believe in magic.

2 · LIVE YOUR PRIORITIES

WHILE TEACHING ON a Greek island several years ago, I led an inner journey for people to meet a blockage. A young man came up to me after the workshop, and said he had imagined walking towards the end of a pier but felt too frightened to complete the inner journey. He explained that he was HIV-positive, and his future looked uncertain – so I took him through the inner journey on his own. There was a pavilion at the end of the pier, and he felt sure that Death was waiting for him inside. I encouraged him to go inside – holding his hands, which were shaking with fear. He hesitated, then found the courage to go in. There stood a dark, hooded figure. He asked Death why she was there, and Death said to him, 'I have come as your friend. You have been afraid of life – living a half-life, limited by fear. But now that I am here, you fear me instead. *Now* will you begin to live your life?'

At workshops, I sometimes ask people to imagine that they have two years left to live. You will be in perfect health until you die – and money is not a particular problem. What will you do? How will you spend your time? Your answer might highlight areas of your life which are out of balance, or which you have been ignoring or postponing. Some people realise that they have paid too little attention to their loved ones; others say they would travel the world, or pursue a new hobby, or go on retreat; some become aware of unfinished business which they need to resolve; and yet others decide that they would change their career, or write that novel, or train in feng shui, or volunteer in a hospice. (No one, as far as I'm aware, has said that they would watch more TV, or do more shopping – yet research shows that this is how most people spend the majority of their leisure time!)

Very few people would change nothing if they had only a year or two to live. Most of us treat our everyday lives as if we will be here forever – and it sometimes takes a life-threatening illness, or the death of a friend, or some other trauma before we really, honestly, truly take in the fact that *you and I are going to die.* Our time on Earth is limited and hugely precious. It's worth trying to absorb this fact *without* having to create a crisis! Shamans refer to death as 'the wise advisor', since facing our death means that we start appreciating *life*, instead of taking it for granted.

What matters most to you? Are you giving enough time and energy to your primary relationships, children, friends, work, creativity, spiritual growth, adventure, your body and health, your home, time for yourself? Why not design your life now to reflect your true priorities – so that when you face death you will have no regrets, no unfinished business, no unfulfilled hopes and dreams? (Who knows, you *might* only have a year or two to live. There are no guarantees.)

I spend my time wisely, knowing it is precious.

3 · If It Feels Heavy, Don't Do It!

SEVERAL YEARS AGO, after the publication of *Living Magically* and *Stepping into the Magic*, I received up to 10,000 letters and phone-calls each year – and answered each one personally. I also led countless workshops, gave talks, recorded self-help tapes and ran my mail-order business single-handed. I was working up to 90 hours per week – so, not surprisingly, I felt exhausted and burnt-out. Yet I had such a strong sense of duty and commitment that I felt obliged to answer every letter in detail, or even phone to offer free telephone counselling. Looking back, it was quite crazy!

Eventually, after many nudges from Spirit, I took a 3-day silent retreat in a cottage on the Yorkshire moors to reflect on my life. I clarified what I really loved doing, and what made me feel heavy and resistant, or seemed a waste of time. It was clear what I needed to do. On arriving home, I 'filed' several boxes of unanswered mail, which I had read, into black binbags – and threw them out. To my surprise, no bolt of lightning struck me down! I also cut down hugely on my work commitments, to create some time for *me* – and took on secretarial help. It transformed my life. I had far more time to do the work I really love – *and* I freed myself up enough to fall in love and get married.

The spiritual law – which I had been foolishly ignoring – is to 'follow your energy'. If someone asks you to do something, and it makes your heart sink, then say No. In ways you might not understand, you'll be doing them and yourself a favour. Perhaps they need to do it themselves, or to ask someone else; maybe it isn't right for them, or they are setting you up as a rescuer, which will keep them stuck in the role of victim. (Interestingly, once I stopped replying to letters, many people wrote to say that just writing a letter had helped them to clarify issues, or gain their own insights. They hadn't needed a reply anyway – or had moved on by the time they heard from me.)

As soon as you catch yourself thinking, 'I really *should* do this', or worrying about what someone will think if you say no, you're listening to the Hard Time voice of guilt, duty and obligation. That part of you is doing its best, bless its little cotton socks, but it doesn't understand the spiritual laws of the universe. The word 'should' never comes from our higher Self; it comes from the part of us which feels unworthy, undeserving and guilt-ridden (or which prides itself on being indispensable, irreplaceable or saint-like).

Why go to a dinner party with people you find dreary or incompatible? Or take your children to a theme park when you cringe at the prospect? Say no – and make space for someone else at the dinner table, or for a friend or relative to take your children. Everyone will be much happier. If it's something which really *has* to be done – such as filling in your tax return, or doing the ironing – then either wait until you feel like doing it (yes, it can happen!), or 'see the bigger picture' (*see Chapter 10*), or somehow make it fun. Or delegate it to someone else: pay someone to do the ironing, or get an accountant to fill in your tax return. (If you tell yourself you can't afford this, see the section on *Money*!)

If it feels heavy, don't do it! It's a rule which gives an amazing sense of freedom to life. It allows you to devote your time and energy to people, work and activities that you truly love. Best of all, it is a powerful tool for letting go of struggle and living in Soft Time.

I follow my bliss.

4 · ALLOW OODLES OF MOODLING TIME

MOODLING MEANS IDLE pottering, dawdling and dreaming, doing nothing in particular, without any goal or purpose. In her lovely book *If You Want to Write*, Brenda Ueland observes that people who are always dashing about 'as busy as waltzing mice', who never allow themselves to slow down, tend to have 'little, sharp, staccato ideas' – whereas those who allow generous periods of moodling time have 'slow, big ideas'. It's a lovely description of the difference between Hard Time and Soft Time.

If you're used to living in Hard Time, then moodling will feel like wasted time, and a little voice will whine and nag that you have so much to *do*! Our ego-self tends to confuse being busy-busy with being valued and important – but chronic busyness is pointless and self-defeating. The reality is that our 'in tray' will never be empty. There will always be countless tasks which you need or want to complete – so if you wait until you've done everything before slowing down the pace of your life, you'll still be waiting to relax when you're on your deathbed. (Or your body-mind or natural Self might get so fed up that it will *force* you to slow down – through serious illness or an accident.)

Moodling time might include staring out of the window,

a long soak in the bath, pottering in the garden, leafing idly through magazines, watching a river flow, gazing into a flickering fire, sitting on a park bench or watching children play. The key to moodling is that it allows you to switch off your 'busy' self, and shift into Soft Time. (If you're worrying about what you *should* be doing, or fretting about your problems, you're not moodling.) Mooding always feels deliciously pleasant, and has an air of timelessness; and it usually involves silence and solitude – essential as they are to a soul-ful life.

If you find it quite impossible to 'sit and do nothing', then do something relaxing and pleasurable such as walking, sailing, horseriding, baking cakes, sketching or embroidery – or even ironing or decorating, if you find it relaxing – but (and this is crucial) take it at a v-e-r-y s-l-o-w p-a-c-e, so that you have plenty of time to dream and ponder. Or you can go for a long solitary walk in order to reflect on an issue, or to ask for inspiration.

One possibility is to tithe 10 per cent of your day to Soft Time – that's 2–3 hours per day. (If you miss a day or two, you can always make up for it later – perhaps with a whole day of moodling.) I call it Goddess time – time for 'simply being'.

Moodling might seem pointless to our rational mind, but it gives us access to our feminine energy, to our 90 per cent mind – our source of vision, inspiration, purpose and higher guidance. It also helps us to live in the here-and-now. As Ram Dass, the famous spiritual teacher puts it, 'For an ounce of doing good, you need a pound of sitting still.' Why not start right now?

I allow time for simply 'being'.

5 · SIMPLIFY YOUR LIFE

JOAN BREEZED INTO my consulting room in an expensive-looking tailored suit, high-heeled shoes and bright red lipstick. She ran a successful PR company, had two teenage children, 'worked out' in a gym three times a week – and came to see me because she was thoroughly depressed. 'I grew up believing that if only I worked hard and was successful, I could have everything I wanted – and I would be happy', she told me. 'But here I am, envied by lots of people – and some days, I just want to die'. Like many overachievers, Joan felt out of control of her life. She was addicted to the adrenalin rush of constant busyness and deadlines – she kept glancing nervously at her watch – and didn't know how to get off the merry-go-round. She wore a bright, winning smile on the outside – but inside, she felt numb. Her children rarely saw her, and she began to dream about selling her company and living a quieter, simpler life – before it was too late.

Our ego-self tries to kid us that happiness lies 'out there' – in success, wealth, power, possessions or romance. Deep down, we all know that this isn't true, yet most of us have been seduced by the false promises of Hard Time – working harder, buying more, aiming higher, taking on even more commitments, or searching for that mythical soulmate who will transform our lives. We end up juggling so many demands and roles that it is impossible to relax and enjoy life.

Similarly, we can feel exhausted by having clutter around us.[1] There are huge pressures on 'consumers' to spend, spend, spend, and our homes are often full of objects we don't really want or need, which merely complicate our lives, muddy our thinking and distract us from our priorities. (Before you buy anything, it's worth asking yourself: 'Will this really add to the quality of my life? Do I *really* want it? Or will it just add to the clutter in my home or office?')

As we shift into Soft Time, we know that enough is enough. We develop greater clarity about our higher purpose and priorities, and often yearn for a simpler, more balanced life. This doesn't necessarily mean living in a wooden shack with no running water or electricity – but it does mean letting go of clutter and details which weigh us down, and being much more choosy about how we spend our time and money. When our *outer* world is simpler, our *inner* world of thoughts and feelings tends to be simpler too – and (as I know from my own experience) with a slower pace of life, it becomes easier to see what really matters, and to enjoy the simple pleasures of life.

If you feel an inner pull towards simplicity, grab a pen and paper, and 'go within'; then ask your higher wisdom: 'What do I need to do to simplify my life?' Be open to the possibility of making big changes – such as moving to a smaller home, leaving the city, resigning from your job or going part-time, or throwing out your entire wardrobe. Or you might feel moved to take small, easy steps at first — such as not listening to the news, shopping less often or limiting your wardrobe to two or three basic colours which suit you. Trust your heart — and take action!

I enjoy the simple pleasures of life.

6 · LEARN TO SAY 'AH WELL!'

MY BROTHER HAS a converted barn in France which was just a shell when he bought it – so he employed a stream of builders, plumbers and other workmen to help make it habitable. There seemed to be one disaster after another – from a supporting wall collapsing to a flood while the electrics were being wired up – yet he noticed that the workmen tended to shrug, smile and say 'Ah well!' After a while, it rubbed off – and my brother found that he too was shrugging off a crisis, and saying 'Ah well!'.

Learning to say 'Ah well!' is an invaluable ability. When something goes wrong – whether it's as trivial as a broken plate or a flat tyre, or as serious as redundancy or a tree collapsing on your house – you have a choice about how to respond. You can panic and awful-ise the situation, and generally feel sorry for yourself – like a teenager with a spot on their chin who thinks the world has come to an end – or you can choose to say 'Ah well!'

As the mother of a toddler, I often find myself saying 'Ah well!' when my newly clean-and-tidy kitchen is ransacked, the floor is covered with pans, spoons and table mats, yogurt is poured on to the carpet and carefully trodden in, and while I'm clearing up *that* mess, a packet of cereal is tipped vigorously into the washing machine – all amidst whoops of delight from a little one! (Children offer count-less opportunities to develop patience, tolerance and a sense of humour!)

More seriously, when I first heard that my father had bowel cancer, I knew that I had a choice. I could worry endlessly about him and my mother, weep and wail and fear that he was soon going to die – or I could say a huge 'Ah well!', send loving and positive thoughts, and know that (whatever happened) it would all be OK. I chose the latter – and it helped me maintain my inner peace to a remarkable extent during this family crisis. (Two years on, he is clear of cancer and enjoying life immensely.)

Another useful expression is 'EWOP', which stands for Everything Works Out Perfectly.[2] If you have just missed your train or plane, or the job you wanted is offered to someone else, or you are made redundant, or someone ends a relationship with you, or your best friend moves to another city – say EWOP (and believe it). It does help shift you into an expanded state of awareness.

Saying 'Ah well!' or EWOP does not mean resigning yourself to a bad situation, or denying your feelings. It is an attitude of acceptance and genuine trust. It means *accepting* what has happened (so that you can go forward from there), *trusting* that you can deal with it, and *knowing* that – since we live in a friendly universe – it will all turn out for the best in the end. It is a way of moving – instantly – into Soft Time.

I am at peace with myself – whatever happens.

7 · FOCUS ON THE POSITIVE

WE GET WHAT we focus upon. This is one of the basic laws of our universe, which mystics have known about for thousands of years. Our thoughts and emotions are like magnets which draw certain people, events and situations towards us, and push others away – so that the outer world 'magically' comes to reflect our inner world. This is why Hard Time and Soft Time are both self-fulfilling prophecies.

Every thought is a prayer. If your thoughts are positive ones – about the people you love, the Dreams you are moving towards and all that is good in your life – then you attract more of the same. If your thoughts are mostly negative or fear-laden – about the leaking roof, your almost-empty bank account, your moody teenager, the slipping clutch in your car, your demanding mother-in-law, that nagging pain in your stomach – then likewise, you attract more of the same.

If you really *have* to be negative, then give yourself a ten-minute stint of nothing-but-worrying-and-whinging, and get it out of your system! Worry about everything that just might happen, put the worst possible interpretation on what *has* happened, and for good measure, grab this opportunity to whinge, whine, blame and generally complain about your life. Don't allow yourself a single positive thought. Hopefully you'll soon start giggling – and I can almost guarantee that you won't last the full ten minutes. (If you do, and it just feels like your usual thoughts, then you really *do* have problems!)

Of course, it can be helpful to contemplate a problem, to understand it from a larger perspective, to ask 'What's *really* going on here?' – free from any blame or shame. That can lead to an 'Aha!' experience of insight which can transform how we see and approach a situation. It is quite different from pointless circular worry and chitter-chatter about a problem, which merely stokes the fire.

If you worry a lot, it is worth having a chat with The Worrier within you. In its own way, it's doing its best to be helpful – perhaps trying to protect you from shock or disappointment by 'preparing you for the worst', or believing that if only you worry enough, you might figure out a solution. You could explain to that part of you that we get what we focus on, so worry only attracts more problems – and that it is often when we *let go* of a problem that we see a way through, rather than when we gnaw at it like a bone. Ask The Worrier to worry about what you *want* to happen instead – your Dreams for the future – so that it can help rather than hinder you. (*Also see Chapter 8.*)

If you take a positive attitude towards life, then whatever happens you will make the best of the situation – seeing the opportunity in every crisis, always asking yourself 'What can I learn from this?' or 'What is the gift in this situation?'. (It might not *seem* as if there's a 'gift' in your flooded kitchen or unexpected redundancy or migraine – but I can promise you there is.)

It's also worth noticing what goes through your mind before you go to sleep. This is a powerful time, when your subconscious mind is very open to suggestion. Do you worry about your problems? Or focus on the mundane details of your life, and what needs to be done? Or look for the 'gifts' in your everyday experiences? Or feel gratitude for all that is good and right in your life – and dream about your Dreams? We get what we focus upon – so focus on the positive.

I focus on what is good and right in my life.

8 · DEAL WITH WHAT IS, NOT WHAT MIGHT BE

WHEN WE'RE IN Hard Time we feel unsafe in the world, so our ego-self tends to worry about what *might* happen – and imagine the worst. It is prone to what Richard Carlson[3] calls 'thought attacks'. Let's suppose that you've just started a promising relationship with Chris, who has promised to phone at 8 o'clock. Your ego-self watches the clock, and when 8 o'clock passes and the phone doesn't ring, it starts to run anxiously through all the potential reasons why. It settles for the worst possible scenarios: either Chris has had a terrible accident, or has decided the relationship is over. Within an hour, you are exhausted with worry and depression, wondering why your relationships never work out and how come you are 'unlovable'. It is a full-blown thought attack! Then Chris phones full of apologies, having been held up in traffic. Thanks to the ego, you've suffered an hour of *angst* over nothing.

The ego is not good at living in the present moment. It is accustomed to fear, anxiety, struggle and melodrama, and tends to project into the future looking for possible problems. Struggle can feel familiar and strangely comforting, like a well-worn boot, so our ego-self often feels uneasy when life is going well – and looks for *something* to worry about.

Much of our stress and anxiety comes from worrying about what *might* happen: What if your house burns down? What if you lose your job? What if your child dies? What if your spouse has an affair? What if you are attacked in a dark alley? What if your headache is a brain tumour? What if a giant hogweed gobbles up your home . . .? Or analysing to death what *has* happened: What did your boss *really* mean by, 'We'll have a review of your work next month'? Why isn't your child eating properly? Why did your husband peck his secretary on the cheek at Christmas?

Right here, in this present moment, there is rarely any genuine stress. It is all in our minds. Like the monk who dangles below the tiger, we *can* choose to focus on the delicious strawberry (see p. 9) – which is here, now – or we can project ourselves into an imagined past or future, and be thoroughly miserable.

When a friend discovered a fungal growth in her cellar, her mind immediately started to race. She imagined a specialist shaking his head and murmuring 'dry rot', 'seems to be everywhere', 'should have caught it earlier' – and saw her life savings disappearing, then having to sell the house at a huge loss. Her whole life was collapsing at the sight of a small fungus! Then she caught herself, and said, 'Stop it! All you know for sure is that there's some fungus in the cellar – so call someone in and find out more'. Then she shifted back into the present moment – and was able to take positive action. (It *was* dry rot, but was handled surprisingly easily and cheaply.) By dealing with what actually is, rather than what might be, we can save ourselves a huge amount of stress.

The present moment is our point of power. In English,

the word 'present' also means 'a gift' – while in the Hawaiian language, *ano* means present moment, peaceful, holy and sacred. This moment is a sacred gift – and if we stay focused in the moment, even during a crisis, we will be living in Soft Time.

I focus on what is happening now.

9 · DELETE 'YES BUT ...' & 'CAN'T...' FROM YOUR VOCABULARY

'I'D LOVE TO travel round the world for a year – if only I could afford it.'

'So why don't you sell your house?'

'Yes, but where would I live when I stopped travelling?'

'Rent a home – or buy a smaller house?'

'Yes, but I couldn't resign from my job.'

'Why not? You could get another job.'

'Yes, but I couldn't possibly abandon my parents/grown-up children for a year.' (Or take my children out of school, or whatever.) And so on, *ad nauseam* . . .

Whenever you have a 'Yes-but' discussion like this, the reality is that you're *scared* of following your Dream. After all, it might change you. It might liberate you. You might hate it. You might feel lonely. You might have to face hidden parts of yourself. You might get into situations that you're unsure how to handle. So – be honest with yourself. If you hear yourself 'Yes-butting', ask yourself what's *really* going on. What are your fears? And if your big Self wants to do something, but your little Self feels scared or insecure, how might you reassure those frightened parts of yourself? (After all, whatever happens, you have created it – and you can handle it.)

When we're living in Hard Time, certain phrases crop up again and again – phrases which get in the way of living with joy and fulfilling our higher purpose, which drag us down into heaviness, stuckness and frustration. 'Yes, but . . .' is perhaps the most insidious phrase, since it can sound so *reasonable* – as if you're just being sensible and thinking things through. It can become a habitual way of blocking yourself from change and growth. It is also one of the most irritating phrases for friends, family and colleagues – who might be doing their best to support and encourage you!

Another common way of blocking growth and change is saying 'I can't . . .': I can't sing/can't dance/can't sell my house/can't leave my partner/can't live alone/can't afford to work part-time/can't leave my job/can't find like-minded friends/can't move out of the city/can't go to college/can't . . . Oh yes, you can! If you have a heartfelt desire to do anything, you *can* do it – in time. There is almost always a way. The reality is that you are *choosing* not to do it, at least for the time being.

Listen to yourself for the next few weeks. Do you justify and rationalise your stuckness by saying 'Yes but . . .'? Do you limit and disempower yourself by saying 'I can't'? Or do you use other Hard Time phrases such as 'If only . . .', 'What if . . .', 'I ought to . . .', 'I haven't got time' or 'I'll try . . .'? Why not replace your Hard Time vocabulary with positive phrases from Soft Time, such as:

- I could . . .
- I choose to . . .
- I choose not to . . .
- I will . . .

– and notice whether you begin to feel, think and choose differently as a result.

I can do anything I really want to do.

10 · See the Bigger Picture

A CLIENT OF mine used to devote her days to making her house sparkle. She dusted, vacuumed, emptied bins, cleaned the bathroom and scrubbed the kitchen floor at least once a day, plumped up cushions as soon as someone rose from the chair, and chased her toddler anxiously with a damp cloth. Needless to say, she didn't *enjoy* her child's early years, because she was too busy trying to keep the house clean. If you had asked her *why* it was so important to clean the house all day long, she would have been puzzled: doesn't *everyone* want a spotless house? But looking back, she wished she had relaxed and spent more time with her child.

There are times in everyone's life when you lose perspective on what really matters, when you 'can't see the forest for the trees'. There are three main reasons:

• Sometimes it means that your inner Child, your natural self, is hurting – and one way to keep painful feelings at bay is to be busy-busy, and give yourself lots to think about. Emotions tend to move much more slowly than thoughts, and take time to bubble up – so if you move fast enough, they might not catch you! But you pay a price for this. It's tiring to run away from yourself – and eventually it takes its toll on your health and well-being.

• Sometimes you might lose your way because your ego-self has taken over, and you're focusing on details rather than on what really matters – like hospital staff who behave as if everything would be fine if it weren't for the patients, or teachers who secretly think that the only 'problem' is the pupils.

• Or it might be that you never *had* a bigger picture – that you have no idea what your higher purpose is, or what your Dreams are – so you choose a 'false goal' in order to have *something* to aim for, rather like an anorexic who aims to be thinner and thinner without really knowing why.

If you ever find yourself lost in busywork – reading junk mail, ironing your undies, rearranging pens on your desk, cleaning a spotless bath, mowing a lawn which looks like a bowling green, or aimlessly surfing the Internet – stop and ask yourself what is going on? Are you avoiding something? Painful feelings? Or a dawning insight that scares you? Or is your life lacking in direction and purpose? Do you really have nothing better to do?

A question I often ask myself is: 'What is the bigger picture here?' *Whatever* you are doing, ask yourself whether it is part of your Dreams or higher purpose, *or* is a way of expressing or developing a higher quality such as love or gratitude, *or* whether you are simply enjoying it, *or* whether it is truly essential? If the answer is No to all of these, then why *are* you doing it?

Seeing the bigger picture is often the key to a more positive attitude to *whatever* you are doing – from washing the dishes to getting to work on time.

There is a story about a scientist working late at NASA space station in the early 1970s. He happened upon a cleaning woman scrubbing the floor earnestly, long after the other cleaning staff had gone home — and asked what she was doing there. She looked at him in surprise, and said: 'I'm putting a man on the moon.' Now *that's* seeing the bigger picture!

I open up to the bigger picture.

11 · Take Responsibility – Not Blame – for Your Life

A FEW YEARS ago, an old schoolfriend of mine had cancer – and asked me to send my tapes on *The Magic of Health*, and an article I wrote on the psychology of cancer. I did so – along with a personal letter outlining some issues she might want to think about, given what I knew about her life and why people get cancer. She was deeply upset by my letter, saying that I was 'blaming' her for having cancer and making out it was 'all her fault', as if she didn't feel bad enough already – and promptly cut off all contact with me. I felt devastated, and sickened that I had increased her stress – but also puzzled, since she was aware of my beliefs and had seemed to want to know more.

I soon realised that I had been caught in a 'drama triangle', in which someone (the victim) asks for help, someone else offers it (the rescuer/martyr), and the victim then switches to the role of persecutor, making the rescuer feel bad. It's an all-too-common game of shame-and-blame tactics. She was understandably angry at her situation, and I was the fall-guy. In order to attract this, I had to be playing the martyr; and indeed I had been, since I had been 'over-whelmed with demands' that week – a sure sign of martyrhood! – but somehow found time to write my friend a long letter, more from a sense of obligation than from love, which is why it backfired.

It illustrated well for me one of the 'pitfalls' of metaphysics, especially for beginners – that taking 100 per cent *responsibility* for your life can be misinterpreted as *taking the blame*. The former is empowering; the latter is disempowering and non-mystical.

The whole idea of taking responsibility is that if you feel like a 'poor victim' – of someone else's behaviour, or of bad luck, or genetics, or a disease, or the government – then you are stuck, immobilised, unable to change the situation. If you assume instead that whatever happens, you're creating that reality, then a whole range of options opens up to you. If you created it, you can *un*-create it, or create something else! Exciting! And you must have created it for a *reason*, so you can work out what you were hoping to learn from it. You can also figure out *how* you created it, so that you don't repeat something similar in future. You can learn and grow from the experience. Best of all, you feel there is something you can *do* – that you don't just have to sit back and accept the situation.

Blaming yourself, on the other hand, is a way of staying stuck. 'Oh, stupid me – look at what I've created!' It is a way of beating yourself up, of criticising your inner Child, of wallowing in guilt. It makes you feel heavy and resentful and frustrated. It increases inner conflict, and makes it much more difficult to work out what is going on, and what to do about it.

If you catch yourself getting into self-blame, then stop yourself: 'Hang on, I'm blaming myself at a time when I need to be especially kind and gentle with myself. I've created this situation and it feels bad – but I'm going to work on it, and make things better'.

Taking responsibility for your life – whatever happens – is always helpful. Taking the blame is a no-no!

I joyfully take responsibility for my life.

12 · GIVE YOUR PROBLEMS TO SOFT TIME

ONE OF MY favourite uses of Soft Time is to give it problems to solve! If you have an issue which you have considered, analysed and generally strangled to death – and *still* you can't come up with a solution – then you need to give it to Soft Time.

My husband and I recently puzzled for a year or so over our housing situation. We rent a 400-year-old house with a stunning garden in the heart of the Lake District, which feels very much like 'home' – yet we also wanted a 'home of our own', so that we could eventually retire without huge monthly outgoings on rent. What's more, we both had a heartfelt Dream of owning a *second* home in Cornwall! We viewed several properties in the Lakes, feeling disheartened at how much we would have to pay – and depressed at the thought of moving house. We couldn't decide what to do.

Then I gave the problem to Soft Time – and within a few days, a magical solution bubbled up: 'Stay where you are, and buy a cottage in Cornwall. That way, you can settle down in the rented home you love, *and* have an affordable house of your own, *and* a second home to enjoy – all for much less than it would cost to buy a house in the Lakes'. (Our rational minds had believed that we had to own a 'first' home before we could buy a 'second'.) It seems obvious now, but it was a revelation at the time. Shortly afterwards, we bought our lovely whitewashed Cornish cottage.

Our '10 per cent mind' – our rational, analytical mind – is only designed to cope with a limited range of problems and decisions. If you need to convert a loft, or buy a new computer, then your rational mind can help you research the options, weigh up the pros and cons, and make a decision. It is excellent for planning, organising and taking action.

However, the big questions in life are rarely suited to rational thinking: 'Why can't I find a soulmate?' 'What is my life purpose?' 'How do I heal my marriage?' 'Why do I have this health problem?' 'Why do I never have any money?' Our 10 per cent mind cannot answer questions like this. It goes into 'analysis paralysis', and we get stuck.

The rule is: if you're struggling with an issue, you're in Hard Time – so stop! Your 90 per cent mind has access to far more information than your conscious ego-self, and can come up with amazingly creative, sometimes wacky solutions which often neatly solve several problems at once.

To give a problem to Soft Time: firstly, trust that there is *always* a solution to any problem, and admit that you don't know what it is – so that your rational mind lets go. Stop struggling and say, 'I'm giving this problem to Soft Time', or write the question on a piece of paper, and put it in a special place reserved for Soft Time questions. Secondly, be patient. Sometimes I've had a striking answer within five minutes, but it might take hours, days or weeks. (Our '90 per cent mind' operates beyond linear time, so *it* comes up with a solution instantly. The delay is at our end!) Eventually you might have a sudden 'Aha!' experience, or a dawning awareness of what you need to do – either when you're ready to hear it, or when the timing is right, or when you give yourself enough moodling time for it to bubble up. Often the solution is simple and obvious – but somehow you had never thought of it before. That is the magic of Soft Time.

I trust that there is always a solution.

13 · Own Your Shadow

OVER THE YEARS, we all tuck away aspects of ourselves which we feel are bad, shameful, painful, scary, inappropriate or unacceptable – perhaps our tears, anger, envy, grief, painful memories, or certain desires or longings. Our Shadow is rarely as fearful and hideous as we imagine it to be – and it often holds 'nuggets of gold' such as our courage, laughter, creativity and joy, since we often grow up feeling embarrassed about our best and highest qualities. Sooner or later, we need to reclaim these lost parts of our wholeness: our dark and light Shadow.

If you look at your strongest or weakest qualities, the opposite probably lies in your Shadow – such as the extrovert with a introvert Shadow, or the pacifist with an aggressive Shadow. Or if you consider what you admire in others, or what irritates you most, you can be sure that those qualities belong to your Shadow Self.

It is risky to suppress parts of ourselves. It creates inner conflict, and reduces our energy and vitality. It can make us seem two-dimensional to other people. It can make us ill, since our body-mind has to express what we are denying. Or we might get our partner or children to 'act out' our Shadow for us. (Are your teenagers doing anything you abhor – getting drunk, sleeping around, dying their hair green? Does your partner drive you crazy by being so untidy, or cynical, or lazy, or arrogant, or distancing? If so, might they be acting out your Shadow?)

Our Shadow can even leak out in horribly antisocial ways. Most psychotherapists – myself included – have seen clients who were molested by priests, whose sexuality has been denied and distorted; or there are meek, mild-mannered people who explode into violent rage after years of suppressing anger. Our 'dark' side isn't necessarily bad, but it can become so if it is completely denied. Dark just means hidden from the light; it simply needs to be owned, so that its gifts can be released.

Honouring your Shadow does not mean you have to act it out, fully and completely. It means allowing yourself to come into balance – so if you're a health food freak, you probably need to have an occasional slice of chocolate gateau; if you're a pacifist, you need to own and honour your anger, and see its positive side; and if you're always oh-so-nice to everyone, why not allow yourself a 'nasty' morning once in a while, even if you just swear at a wall! As Jung noted, extremes tend to turn into their opposites – so we need to acknowledge our 'other side'.

Post-modern theologian Matthew Fox tells a lovely story about a woman who always seemed genuinely joyful. He asked her 'how come?' – and she told him her secret. Once a year, she went potholing down the deepest, darkest cave she could find – and stayed there in pitch blackness for three whole days. In that time, she faced all of her inner demons – and was able to emerge into the light feeling joyous and whole again.

We don't all have to go potholing – but we do need to face our inner demons. As we shift into Soft Time, this becomes a more natural and easy process. We stop judging ourselves (and others) for being human, give up the need to be 'perfect', and feel more at ease with our emotions, contradictions and inadequacies. This self-love also unblocks the pathway to our inner wisdom, psychic abilities and higher qualities – our Light Shadow. (In Huna terms, we are more fully connected with our basic/natural Self and our higher Self.) As an embodied mystic, we become both more human and ordinary *and* more 'divine' and extraordinary. By facing up to our inner demons, we also give birth to the angel within us.

I honour every part of my wholeness.

14 · LET GO OF YOUR ADDICTIONS

WE LIVE IN an addictive society – that is, a society which encourages us to look outside the Self for happiness and fulfilment (rather like searching for God in all the wrong places). Most of us have at least one addictive way of coping with life: perhaps overworking, alcohol, drugs, overeating, dieting, shopping, TV-watching, busyness, smoking, exercise or staring at a computer screen. Addiction is a way of getting a brief 'high' or numbing ourselves emotionally (perhaps stuffing down anger with a packet of biscuits, or suppressing tears with a cigarette), which becomes a habitual way of dealing with stress. Since our society considers it 'normal' to shop compulsively for goods we don't need, or to watch television for hours each day, many people are unaware that these can be unhealthy and self-destructive addictions which cut us off from our deep Self.

The first step in overcoming addiction is to be honest with yourself, and admit you have a problem. In the early stages of addiction, most of us deny that anything is wrong: 'I just love my work', 'I like being skinny', 'I just enjoy smoking', 'I thrive on being busy', or 'My boss just expects a lot'. Or we kid ourselves that our favourite addictive behaviour is 'healthy' – such as meditating or reading – and therefore couldn't possibly pose any difficulty. However, most addictions grow over time – sometimes slowly, over many years – and all too often, an addict's life is a mess by the time they admit to a problem. So start by looking at yourself honestly in the mirror.

Then work out how your addiction is serving you. Is it a way of avoiding emotions or intimacy? A way of 'coping' with a lifestyle that you need to change? A way of shutting your ears to higher guidance, or cutting yourself off from your body? A way of comforting or rewarding yourself? A way of boosting your self-esteem? (Look at what is happening and how you are feeling each time you dive towards the fridge or switch on your computer: is there a pattern?)

Then ask yourself whether you could meet those needs, or change your lifestyle, or deal with your fears, or honour your emotions and longings in healthier ways. Give yourself plenty of silence and solitude so that you can reconnect with your deep Self.

Addiction is always a sign that our masculine energy is out of balance – that we are being 'driven', and have lost sight of our higher purpose or vision. To overcome addiction, it's essential to follow your Dreams and visions, so that you have a healthy focus for your masculine energy. 'Follow your Dreams' might seem to imply that happiness *can* be found outside the Self – but the point in having Dreams is that it sets us off on a journey. It is the process that matters, not the goal. A truly heartfelt Dream comes from our higher Self, which knows exactly what we need in order to learn and grow; it urges us to search for God (or wholeness) in the *right* places.

Letting go of addiction need not be a prolonged and

painful process. It can be easy and natural. As we shift into Soft Time, the 'pull' towards our old addictions becomes weaker and weaker – and we find ourselves making new choices which support balance, wholeness and joy. That familiar old feeling of being hurried, anxious and 'driven' fades into the past. (I know – I've been there!) We relax into the pure bliss of loving life as it is, while also moving – as gently and effortlessly as a summer breeze – towards the fulfilment of our Dreams.

I relax – and connect with my higher Self.

15 · TRUST YOURSELF

DURING ONE PRIVATE consultation, I received an impression of a small, powerful woman in a beaded white dress standing behind my client – along with the words 'Maori' and 'Lela'. I asked my client whether she knew anything about her guides and she said, 'Well – I'm not sure. In inner journeys, I sometimes see a woman in a white dress who might be Maori. But I don't know – I'm probably just making it up'. When I shared what I had sensed about her guide, she was amazed. Our descriptions matched exactly – and she too had been given the name Lela, and dismissed it. This client had strong intuitive hunches – about what to do, about other people, even about world events – but rarely trusted them. Her guide had sent her to me so that she would learn to trust her intuition.

The age of gurus is coming to an end. It is no longer appropriate for us to turn to priests, seers and other external guides for advice about what to do, or to put others on pedestals and project our wisdom on to them. It is time to trust our own inner guidance, our deep Self. (This is the true meaning of the 'second coming of Christ': the discovery of the Christ within.) Professional psychics and mediums often say that everyone is psychic; the main difference is that they *trust* the fleeting inner impressions which most of us ignore or dismiss.

If we trust our inner wisdom, we know everything we need to know. Almost always, we intuitively *know* what we need to do next, in any area of our lives. It seems like the obvious thing to do – and usually feels joyful and exciting, if a little scary. Perhaps it comes as a 'gut feeling', a quiet inner voice, a heartfelt desire, or a sudden glimpse of our future self – yet we might ignore that inner guidance for months or even years if we don't trust it enough.

My own experience is that when we trust ourselves, life becomes far more magical. If we take a leap of faith – following our hearts, 'knowing' it is the right step to take – the Universe says *Yes, Yes, Yes!* We have to be willing to let go and to change, and often have to close one door before the next door opens. We might have to live in 'the void' for a while – unsure of our next step, giving ourselves lots of space and being-time, learning to live with our confusion and uncertainty. We also need to be open to the unexpected. We often know only what our next step will be – so we must be willing to take one step at a time, trusting that further guidance will follow. But the rewards that come from trusting our inner guidance can be truly amazing.

Ten years ago, when I resigned from my Health Service post in clinical psychology, I had no income, few savings and a mortgage to pay – yet my inner guidance told me to devote myself to writing my book *Living Magically* full-time. I trusted that I would be led, step by step, wherever I needed to go next. Sure enough, just as I completed the manuscript, former colleagues began to ask what my book was about, so I set up a workshop. Then a radio station in

London somehow 'heard about me' – and my radio interview brought a flood of enquiries. Before I knew it, I had moved to London and was running *Living Magically* workshops – and a publisher had accepted my book. I lived off the proceeds from selling my house for a year or so while I built up my new career. By trusting my inner voice, my life was completely transformed.

I am my own highest authority. I trust my inner voice.

16 · Listen to the Whispers — so the Universe Doesn't Have to Shout

Shamans and mystics have always looked for 'signs' in the natural world. A rock, a cloud, a mosaic of autumn leaves or the fresh trail of a deer could all be messengers from Spirit. Our rational ego-self might dismiss it as superstition, but our deep Self knows that beneath the surface reality, the world of appearance, everything is interconnected and meaningful. The world is full of symbols. Everyday events such as a blocked sink, a speeding fine or dampness in the cellar are often 'whispers' — messages from our deep Self which can nudge us towards our soul's chosen destiny.[4]

When we're living in Hard Time, we tend to ignore the 'whispers' that can help and guide us. We get lost in the busyness of our ego-self and forget that everything is meaningful — so we don't notice the signals to stop, slow down or change direction. We are deaf to the whimpers and cries of our inner Child or physical body, or ignore the gentle voice of our higher wisdom. That is when the wake-up calls can become louder — and louder, and louder — until they finally become shouts and screams. Serious illness, car accidents, divorce, bankruptcy, house fires, floods and other traumas *can* all be signs that we have not been listening to the whispers, and our deep Self has had to take drastic action to grab our attention.

Whenever something unusual, painful or repetitive happens, it is worth asking yourself what the 'whisper' is. (It sometimes helps to interpret the incident as if it were a dream, since this makes us think symbolically.) Notice what you were preoccupied with at the time, since this might be what the 'whisper' relates to.

When a bat fluttered into our kitchen late one night, my husband and I immediately took it as a sign of 'rebirth' – the traditional meaning of bat as a power animal – and noted that we had been discussing major changes in his consultancy work. It felt like a good omen. My first book, *Living Magically*, had a butterfly on the cover – and many people have written to tell me of striking experiences with butterflies while reading the book. Such incidents serve as a heartwarming reminder that we live in a magical reality, and often mean: 'Yes! You're going in the right direction!'

When you're living in Soft Time, meaningful coincidences – what Jung called 'synchronicities' – become more common. You're living from your connected Self, your quantum self, so the world mirrors back this Oneness. You decide to set up a business selling dried flowers, and almost everyone you speak to has been looking for dried flowers! You hear of a book you would like to read; someone mentions the same book to you; then a friend sends it unbidden in the post. You wonder whether to call your baby Jade, and *as you ponder this*, you drive past a shop called 'Jade For Babies'; this happened to someone I know. The synchronicities can become so obvious that it feels as if someone is playing a cosmic joke!

A young woman who attended one of my workshops met her guide, Cassandra, on an inner journey. She wondered if she was 'just making it up', so she asked her guide for a sign that she was real. As she walked home from the workshop, she passed through a long subway in which there was just one word of graffiti, scrawled in huge orange letters: CASSANDRA. Her doubts melted away!

I listen to the whispers — and acknowledge the miracles of life.

17 · FORGIVE YOURSELF

ACCORDING TO THE Huna wisdom, if we feel ashamed or guilty, it can block the channel to our higher Self – so it is crucial to clear shame and guilt from our emotional body. The Huna tradition suggests that the only *legitimate* reason to feel guilty is because you have hurt someone. The more deliberately you have hurt them, the more reason to feel guilty – so you make amends, then let it go.

If you sit quietly, and ask your inner Child what it feels guilty about – then allow any memories or images to come to the surface – you might be amazed at how much emotional baggage you are carrying! Many of us carry guilt about harmless activities such as lying in bed until noon, or eating a box of chocolates, or simply being happy. Our culture reinforces the idea that we are not really *supposed* to enjoy ourselves. (God apparently wouldn't approve!)

It's worth deciding what it is appropriate to feel guilty about. Then if you find yourself getting into guilt over taking leave from work (it's *your* time!), or buying yourself expensive clothes (it's *your* money!), or eating cream cakes (it's *your* body!), you can reassure your inner Child that what you are doing is just fine.

Shame is guilt you feel simply for being – often stemming

from feeling unwanted or unloved as a child, or due to a traumatic birth. If you feel undeserving, unworthy and generally lower down the evolutionary scale than an earwig, then you'll grab *any* excuse to feel ashamed – such as being imperfect or human! You will also feel uncomfortable if you're happy or successful, and ensure that you sabotage yourself.

Releasing shame and guilt is a four-stage process:

1. **Become aware** of what you feel guilty about, and let go of shame or guilt which is inappropriate – by reassuring your inner Child that enjoying yourself, relaxing or being human are *not* reasons to feel bad!

2. **Forgive yourself** for any harmful or hurtful behaviour. This means realising that we are always doing the best we can. If you did something 20 years ago that you still feel bad about, pretend you are a loving friend who knows all about it – and let that friend explain why you did what you did. This isn't meant to justify your behaviour, just to provide an opportunity to understand and forgive yourself – or even better, realise that there is nothing to forgive.

3. **Make amends**, if it is appropriate. Perhaps you need to talk about it with the other person, or apologise, or replace what you broke or forgot to return, or whatever. Or if you've lost touch, or the person is dead, or it feels ridiculous to bring it up, you might imagine talking to them. Or choose some joyful way of making amends that feels right to you, such as making an anonymous donation to charity, or secretly paying for a stranger's lunch in a café.

4. **Let it go!** It is in the past, so don't hang on to it any longer. There is a Buddhist story of two monks who come to a river. A woman is waiting on the riverbank, and asks the monks if they will kindly carry her across the river. One monk immediately does so – and they walk on. The other monk is astonished, since monks are not supposed to touch women – and he is still thinking about it the next day, when he asks his friend how he could have done such a thing. The monk replies, 'I put the woman down at the far side of the river. You are still carrying her now'. Guilt makes us cling to an event long after it should be dead and buried. *Put it down!*

I release the past – and forgive myself.

18 · CHERISH YOURSELF – JUST AS YOU ARE

OUR INNER CHILD is invariably wounded in childhood. Our parents, teachers and guardians do their best, but they are only human and cannot provide unconditional love. Most of us learn that we only get love and approval if we are good, or special, or talented, or bright, or beautiful, or quiet, or do as we're told – and so we feel ashamed. We grow up believing there is *something wrong with us*, and that if only we try hard enough, are good enough, perfect enough, achieve enough, earn enough, are attractive enough, we will be loved. Many of us 'keep trying' until we are 30, 40, 50, 60, 70 – thus condemning ourselves to live in Hard Time, since shame can never be healed by trying to be 'good enough', or 'better than' others, or anything other than who we are.

Our inner Child inhabits a world beyond time, so it remembers comments from childhood as if they were made yesterday: 'You're such a nuisance!' 'Why can't you do *anything* right?' 'You're so stupid/clumsy/lazy/bad!' 'You'll never amount to anything'. The inner Child cannot reason for itself – that is the job of the ego-self – so it simply accepts toxic beliefs as if they were literally true, and stores them as information. 'My eyes are blue, I have long legs – and I'm stupid.' It then goes on to prove such statements are true – sometimes throughout our lives!

Any comments which have emotional impact, or which come from authority figures, make a particularly strong impression on our inner Child. Happily this means that books can be healing, since authors are 'authority figures' to our inner Child. If it says in print that you're OK, maybe you really are! So here it is in black-and-white: **There is nothing wrong with you** – apart perhaps from some false, toxic beliefs about yourself and life, which can be released.

Shame can also be healed by connecting with our inner wisdom. Our higher Self knows that everything is God/dess, that no one is 'better than' or 'less than' anyone else. It is impossible to feel like a miserable earthworm – or to feel arrogant – when you are strongly connected with your higher Self.

According to the Huna wisdom, our higher Self (*aumakua*) loves us unconditionally. (*Aumakua* means 'utterly trustworthy parental spirit'.) *Our* task is to offer unconditional love to our inner Child and body – our natural Self – in the same way. This means never criticising or judging ourselves, correcting any toxic beliefs from childhood, and *cherishing* ourselves: allowing ourselves to live in Soft Time, to love, laugh and be merry.[5] Paradoxically, when we love and accept ourselves as we are, our wounds are healed – and so we begin to grow and change. Our ego-self matures, our inner Child is set free – and we start to embody our higher Self.

If it feels like a challenge to love yourself right now, then pretend! If you *did* really love yourself, what would change? How would you think, feel or behave differently? Then just 'act as if' you loved and cherished yourself – until it becomes more and more real.

I aim not to be perfect, but to be perfectly myself.

19 · LISTEN TO THE VOICE OF LOVE, NOT FEAR

MANY YEARS AGO, while travelling alone in the USA, I found myself in a taxi in downtown Los Angeles at midnight, with three large black men who silently glowered at me in a threatening way. My inner Child felt scared, so I asked my deep Self how to handle the situation – and immediately felt bigger and calmer. I affirmed that I was safe and amongst friends, and sent love and light to the men. Within minutes they began to smile and chat with me, warning me about the dangers of downtown LA, and offering to chaperone me safely on to the Greyhound bus! It was only later that I realised what an amazing transformation I had seen.

Whatever the situation, we can listen to the voice of love or the voice of fear. The voice of love, the voice of our deep Self, connects us with the greater reality of Oneness. It knows that everything 'out there' is an aspect of the Self, and that the universe is friendly and loving. It is the 'still small voice within'. It encourages us to grow, to expand, to reach out, to believe in miracles, to follow our Dreams. (And knowing that the world is filled with ego-selves, it can also warn us about potential dangers, ensuring we are not in the wrong place at the wrong time.)

The voice of fear is the voice of our immature ego-self,

which believes in separateness and isolation, which feels alone and frightened, which tries to puff itself up and feel big, but secretly feels ashamed and inadequate. It is the voice in our head which says 'Don't do it! You don't know what might happen! It's too risky!' or 'You *can't* do it! You'll fail! It will be a catastrophe!' or 'Better the devil you know!' or 'It would be selfish to do it. You should put others' needs first'. Sometimes it appears as the 'discouragement committee':[6] other people who voice your fears and doubts, and warn you of the dangers of following your Dreams.

Since we live in an ego-based society, fear is widespread and powerful. It is a form of 'psychic pollution' which affects us at an energy level even if we're not consciously aware of it. It attracts whatever we fear – so we need to find ways of protecting ourselves, or of releasing fear. Here are a few suggestions:

- Don't squash your fears down, since whatever we resist persists. Become aware of your fears *without identifying with them* – and send love to that fearful part of yourself. When you have a fearful thought or slip into a 'thought attack', smile and call Light to yourself – and choose loving, positive thoughts instead.
- Visualise what you're afraid of – and see yourself coping with it. That way, you won't have to make it happen!
- Recognise that it has already happened. Many fears – such as that of dying in childbirth, losing a child or partner, going blind, falling from a great height, losing your house in a fire – date back to past lifetimes. Relax and ask your deep Self to show you what happened in

that other lifetime; then reassure yourself that this lifetime is different, and your fear belongs to the past.
- Imagine releasing fear and doubt in long slow out-
breaths, while breathing in the light of love and trust
with each breath. Or imagine fear and doubt draining
away each time you pull out the plug in your bath.

Anything which lifts your energy, raises your spirits, relaxes
or inspires you will help you listen to the voice of love. Or
simply ask yourself: 'What is the voice of fear telling me in
this situation? And what does the voice of love have to say?'

I listen to the voice of love.

20 · USE YOUR IMAGINATION

EVERYONE IS IMMENSELY creative. No exceptions. After all, we are creative sparks of All That Is! Nothing comes into being without someone, somewhere, imagining it first – even if that 'someone' is God/dess. Imagination is the source of all. It is the bridge between the visible and invisible realms.

However, our creativity is often squashed in childhood. If a teacher or parent says you're 'no good at drawing' or 'no good at essays', then your inner artist or writer might shrivel up and die; or if you're reprimanded for daydreaming, your inner Dreamer might go into hiding. In our Hard Time society, it is somehow more 'important' to learn the capital of Paraguay than to imagine being a snowflake or a tiger. Yet when Einstein imagined what it would be like to ride on a moonbeam, his dream-ride gave birth to the theory of relativity. As adults, we often have to recover and re-own our precious creativity – and allow our imagination to run wild and free again.

Not everyone taps into their creativity in healthy and positive ways – after all, some people have learnt to express it through crime, or by creating tragedy and melodrama in their lives – but everyone has the *potential* to express their inner Self in hugely satisfying ways that can melt inner blockages, heal our inner Child and even make a positive contribution to the world. Creativity links us to our Source; it is a deeply healing process, a way of giving birth to our deep Self.

If you have a free-flowing creative outlet in your life – wonderful! If not, why not honour your creative self on a regular basis? Devote an evening to writing poetry – or scribble down whatever comes to mind for an hour or so? Or get some poster paints, brushes and huge sheets of plain paper – and just paint, allowing yourself to be surprised at what emerges on the paper. Or work with clay or papier mâché or cloth or whatever grabs your fancy. The only rule is: do not allow your ego-self (or anyone else's ego-self) to *judge* what you produce; simply allow it to be. Or sit and daydream: what would it be like to fly like an eagle, or to be a shooting star, or a flower fairy, or a rain-cloud, or a mountain in the Himalayas? Or imagine time running backwards, or being part of the Big Bang, or creating a solar system.

In your everyday life, keep asking yourself: 'What is an *imaginative* way of approaching this?' Or: 'How would the artist/dreamer within me view this situation?' Or if you want to see auras, or sense energy, or see clairvoyantly, imagine you can already do so – so that you reconnect with your natural Self, which can do all this and much more.

(If you need further inspiration and encouragement, or practical suggestions, I highly recommend Julia Cameron's *The Artist's Way*, Natalie Goldberg's *Writing Down the Bones*, Betty Edwards' *Drawing on the Right Side of the Brain*, or Aviva Gold's *Painting from the Source*. Or re-read some of the children's classics — such as Lewis Carroll's *Alice in Wonderland*, Frances Hodgson Burnett's *The Secret Garden* or Roald Dahl's *Charlie and the Chocolate Factory*.)

Imagination is a gateway to Soft Time. It is a doorway to the soul. It is as vital to the human spirit as breathing is to the body. Without imagination, we are like zombies sleep-walking through life. When we turn the key of our imagination, we become dreamers, map-makers, magicians, artists, co-creators. We open the door to transformation, healing and miracles.

I imagine, I dream, I create. I am an artist.

21 · GO WILD!

RECLAIMING OUR WILD Self is an essential step along the road to living in Soft Time. (*See 'Wild and Free' in Part One.*) Our wild or natural Self is exuberant, passionate, fun, spontaneous, energetic, aware, emotional, intuitive, primal and free. It is often abandoned during the long years of growing up and becoming a 'responsible adult'. If you're not having enough fun in your life, or never feel passionate about anything, or find it hard to make decisions, or feel cut off and disconnected, you have lost touch with your wild Self.

If you have been too 'nice' – too civilised, too controlled – for a long time, releasing your wild Self might feel scary at first. It might bounce back into your life like a coiled spring. Whatever we suppress into our Shadow side can *seem* negative when it starts to seep – or explode – back into awareness. A friend of mine who had been a 'good Catholic girl' all her life amazed everyone – including herself – when she had an obsessive affair with a lecherous neighbour after 12 years of marriage. As she said, it was 'totally out of character'. Her wild Self had finally grabbed her attention! Happily her marriage survived – her husband grew to love her emerging wildness – and she began to release her Wild Woman in more positive and creative ways, taking up flamenco dancing, writing poetry and making earthenware pots.

You might like to take an inner journey – imagining you are in a wild and natural landscape – and meet your wild Self, perhaps in the form of a wise old man or woman, a nature spirit, a fiery dragon, a wizard, a nature child or a powerful adult. Allow yourself to be surprised at what form it might take. Ask your wild Self what you need to know, how you can become more wild and free, what he or she wants from you.[7] (It might 'speak' to you through images, feelings, memories or intuitive hunches, rather than in words.) Let your wild Self teach you how to voice your soul, to sing your passion, to bury your snout in the damp earth.

Or do something *joyfully* physical and sensuous that is unusual for you – *not* 'going for the burn' or pushing yourself, but listening to your body's needs and desires: perhaps having a massage with aromatherapy, or using a jacuzzi, or sleeping beneath the stars. Or spend time alone in wild places. Walk barefoot on Mother Earth, sing to the river, listen to the wind, talk to the hills, dance with the nature spirits – and invite your wild Self back into your life.

Releasing our wildness does not mean losing control. It does not mean acting on every whim or impulse, without considering the consequences. It does not mean taking foolish risks. What it does mean is becoming aware of the emotions, desires, burning passions and 'gut feelings' which lie beneath our civilised surface – and expressing or acting upon impulses which feel really good, even if they are unorthodox, 'selfish', unexpected or break your unspoken family rules. If you feel like dancing in your garden at midnight, or asking your boss for an extra week's holiday, or bathing naked in a cool mountain stream, or galloping a horse along a beach, or spending a day alone in silence, or saying No to a dinner invitation, or bashing pillows to release your hurt or rage, or wearing a clown suit in the high street, what's stopping you? Go wild.

I am wild and passionate.

22 · FEEL GRATITUDE AND APPRECIATION — EVERY DAY

GRATITUDE AND APPRECIATION are essential to living in Soft Time, helping us to focus on the positive aspects of our lives rather than dwell on the negative. Most of us have so much to be grateful for — yet it is all too easy to be preoccupied with our 'problems', and forget to be thankful.

Gratitude is the perfect antidote to feeling sorry for ourselves. Self-pity keeps us stuck in Hard Time, whereas genuine gratitude — not a grovelling, servile, false sense of gratitude but a heartfelt, expansive, rolling wave of love and thankfulness — effortlessly lifts us into the Soft Time cycle. As Meister Eckhart put it, 'If the only prayer you say in your life is "thank you", that would suffice'.

What is more, gratitude is a 'one-step process' for manifesting. It is like a magnet. Whenever we feel grateful — perhaps for loving relationships, prosperity, free time, a helpful friend, good news or peace between nations — we attract more of the same. (In Hawaiian, it is no coincidence that 'bless' also means 'give strength to'.)

Gratitude goes hand-in-hand with appreciation. When did you last say to your partner, child, parents, close friends that you love and appreciate them? It is often only after someone dies that their strengths and good qualities are fully acknowledged by their loved ones. (When an old friend died recently – far too young – I wrote a long letter to his wife in appreciation of all he had taught and given me; sadly, I had never thanked him properly while he was still alive.) Appreciation warms the hearts of the living – a heartfelt letter of thanks can certainly make me glow all day long – so why wait? Appreciate someone now. Like gratitude, it will 'raise your vibrations' and make *you* glow too!

Also, everyone needs to appreciate *themselves* from time to time. Don't forget to pat yourself on the back whenever you complete a task well, meet a challenge, take a courageous step, listen to your inner wisdom, or care lovingly for yourself or others. Many of us were taught as children not to 'boast', so we grow up reluctant to say *anything* positive about ourselves – but self-appreciation is an essential step towards becoming our own best friend. It helps us appreciate others more too.

Here are three suggestions:

- **Keep a gratitude diary.** Each night (or as often as you remember), spend a few moments writing down what you felt grateful for today: a warm hug from a friend, seeing the sun rise, a helpful shopkeeper, the song of a skylark. It is amazing how this simple practice can increase your feelings of gratitude, and help you appreciate everyday life even more.
- **Appreciate a friend.** Send a loving card or unexpected gift to a friend to thank them for 'being there'. Bring some flowers next time you drop in for a coffee. Tell a friend exactly *what* you love about them: their

thoughtfulness, their humour, their honesty, their courage, their enthusiasm.

- **Congratulate yourself.** Look back at your life over the past five years. How have you changed and grown in that time? What have you achieved? What challenges have you faced? How have you made a positive difference to the world, even in the smallest of ways? Give yourself a gift in appreciation – a bouquet of flowers, a lovely notebook, a day in the country. Be honest – tell yourself how wonderful you are!

*I take time to be grateful – **every** day.*

23 · NOURISH YOUR SOUL

WHENEVER I WALK amidst the beauty and majesty of the Lake District – beside the mist-shrouded lakes, beneath the silent presence of mountains, along ancient fell-paths or through sun-dappled forests – I feel my heart expand, my toes curl with pleasure, and my spirits soar. A wild and beautiful landscape is almost as vital as breathing to me. It nourishes my soul.

For everyone, there are activities or experiences which call you Home, which connect you with the very deepest parts of your Self. Perhaps it is listening to Irish folk music, or walking beside the ocean, or horse-riding, or Renaissance art, or the beating of a drum, or writing poetry, or making love, or working with clay, or being with young children, or climbing mountains .... Perhaps there are aspects of your work that make you feel inspired – literally, 'filled with spirit'. Or it might be as simple as candlelight, or silence and solitude, or sitting in your garden. (For me, hearing the cry of gulls sends ripples down my spine; for whatever reasons, it is a sound which resonates with my soul.)

Going on a pilgrimage is also deeply nourishing to the soul. To travel with a sense of the sacred is quite different from being a tourist. It means responding to a deep 'inner call', journeying with mindfulness and opening ourselves to the Spirit of a place. It might mean visiting a well-recognised sacred place or power spot – such as Glastonbury, Avebury, Chartres, Lourdes, Bethlehem, Jerusalem, Mecca, the pyramids of Egypt, the Mayan temples of Mexico, Machu Picchu, Mount Shasta, Sedona, Bali or India. (I spent my 40th birthday at Callanish on the isle of Lewis, visiting the powerful standing stones at midnight.) Or it might mean spending time in a place which feels soul-ful to *you* – perhaps because you have strong past-life connections there – a city, a village, a nation, or a particular beach, forest, valley or mountain range. Traditionally one should arrive slowly – preferably on foot – and with a sense of awe, wonder and gratitude. If it is a relatively small site such as a circle of standing stones, then you might circle around it on arrival; I always circle three times clockwise – then silently ask for permission from the Spirits before entering.

To become a soul-infused personality, we have to invite our soul into our everyday life – and recognise that the soul is not nourished by cheese sandwiches or soap operas or travelling on the underground. It needs experiences of a higher vibration, a more refined essence, which resonate with higher dimensions of reality. It is like organic gardening – all we have to do is provide a healthy living environment, and a plant will flourish. With the right conditions, our soul will become more and more embodied. Without the right nutrients, it might withdraw its energy, leaving just a pilot light behind – enough to keep us alive, and 'going through the motions'.

What nourishes *your* soul? What makes you feel deep-down connected? What makes you feel huge, expansive, joyful? What brings you inner peace and harmony? Imagine you are speaking to your soul, and asking what would help you to become more soul-ful. How do you imagine your soul replies?

I take time to nourish my soul.

24 · SLOW DOWN – AND LIVE IN THE MOMENT

RUSHING AND BUSYNESS are modern addictions. As we try to pack more into each day, we might have the illusion that we're closer to feeling happy and fulfilled. The truth is that we are moving further away. Hurry and haste mean we're being driven by our ego-self, which fondly believes that happiness, security or even love can be found by *doing* enough or *having* enough. The problem is that the ego is always hurrying to 'get there', and constantly chitter-chattering about the past and future. And if we are not living in the moment, we are not really *living* at all.

Until we make space for our deep Self in our lives, until we expand beyond the separateness of our ego-self towards the greater reality of Oneness, the experience of pure bliss or true aliveness will be forever elusive. Our deep Self knows that the main purpose of life is to *live* – not to achieve or acquire or even to make a difference, but *simply to live*. Slowing down the pace of your life does not guarantee living in the moment, but it does make it easier.

Here are five simple ways to slow down and stay in Soft Time:

1. **Aim to do less** – It sounds obvious, but if you stop

aiming to do 'as much as possible', and instead give yourself *comfortable* goals at the start of each day or week, you're far more likely to slip into Soft Time. Just dropping one or two major commitments, or aiming to complete four tasks instead of six, can create enough space to *enjoy* your life. (If you find that other tasks expand to fill the extra time, you need to explore your addiction to busyness. *See Chapter 14.*)

2. **Arrive early** – Do you always pack at the last minute? Do you often catch a train or plane with only moments to spare? Do you try to fit in 'one more job' before dashing to an appointment? If so, you're probably adding a huge amount of stress to your life. (My husband still does this, so I observe its stressful impact on an almost daily basis!) If you always plan to arrive early, and allow for the unexpected, you will feel far calmer and more centred.

3. **Enjoy having to wait** – In a supermarket queue or traffic jam, our Hard Time self drums its fingers impatiently, tut-tuts and frets about the 'wasted time'. Our shoulders tense up, and we feel more and more frustrated. Our Soft Time self simply accepts the situation, smiles and relaxes – enjoying the unexpected 'gift' of a slower pace in the day. The situation is the same – only our awareness is different. (A friend who hated traffic jams decided to keep a tin whistle in his car. After that, whenever he was caught in traffic, he would practise a few tunes. Getting stuck in traffic no longer bothered him – *and* he learnt to play a mean whistle!)

4. **Travel more slowly** – Walk or cycle whenever

possible. It's amazing how walking to a corner shop to buy milk, instead of using the car, can increase our quality of life by *slowing us down*. If you must drive, why not deliberately stay well below the speed limit? Enjoy the journey, rather than dashing to 'get there'.

5. **Bring yourself into the moment** – 'Magic moments' come from being fully present. You might be feeling the soft breeze on your face, smelling a baby's hair or eating a plum – but whatever you are doing, you're not lost in thoughts of the past or future, but fully alive in the here-and-now. Right now: let your thoughts slow down and drift past without grabbing hold of them, and bring yourself into *this* unique moment. What can you see, hear, feel or smell right now? How does your body feel? What is happening around you? Can you feel the magic?

I am alive in this moment — now!

25 · CELEBRATE!

WE ARE ALIVE! Right now, you and I have this beautiful planet on which to play and work and love and laugh and run and dance and dream – or just to sit and contemplate the stars. *Wow!* What an amazing gift!

Whenever we get bogged down in tasks, work, details or trying-to-save-the-world, we can take ourselves much too seriously – and lose the sense of aliveness which comes from living in the moment, and having fun. It's worth remembering that 'Angels fly because they take themselves lightly'.

Children – wonderful teachers as they are – are full of fun and celebration. Just this morning, I was writing a shopping list and my husband was making breakfast, when our young son grabbed us both by the finger in turn, trying to pull us away from our tasks. We resisted him, saying we were busy for a moment. Finally we gave in and asked what he wanted – and discovered that he wanted to *dance*. And so we joyfully danced together – celebrating the start of a new day. (Far more important than shopping lists and breakfast!)

Birthdays, anniversaries, holidays, festivals, success and good news are all essential to celebrate. Don't 'make do' with a card and a gift if it's the birthday of someone special.

Buy balloons, make a banner, decorate the house, serve a feast, make a fuss! If you are offered a new job, invite a few friends around and tell them you want to party! Grab every excuse to celebrate and have fun.

Then there are the festivals of whatever religion you were born into. I love Christmas and Easter (which are, of course, pagan festivals 'borrowed' by Christianity). I also enjoy the traditional Celtic festivals, which are a lovely way to celebrate nature and our connectedness with the Earth – perhaps by lighting candles and incense, preparing a special meal, reciting poetry, dancing, gathering with friends, giving thanks. (The earth energies around solstice and equinox also make them powerful times to reconsider your life, plan the coming months, and make any requests to the Universe for help and support in fulfilling your Dreams.)

The primary Celtic festivals are:

SEPTEMBER 23: Autumn equinox. Nature's New Year. Time to look at the balance of your life, and begin to consider 'what comes next'.

OCTOBER 31: Samhain (pronounced 'Sow-een'). Traditionally when the doorway to the Otherworld is most open. Time to clear our clutter and release the past.

DECEMBER 21: Winter solstice. Celebration of 'return of the light'. Time for going within, to look at your inner self and private life.

FEBRUARY 1: Imbolc. Day of the Goddess Brighid. Herald of

the Spring and new birth. Think about new directions for the coming year.

MARCH 21: Spring equinox. Look at the balance of your life again. Begin to take action on planned projects.

MAY 1: Beltane. Start of the Celtic summer. Celebration of fertility. Doorway to the Otherworld is again wide open.

JUNE 21: Summer solstice. Celebration of co-creation. Give thanks to Mother Earth. Look at your contribution to the world: your 'public self'.

AUGUST 1: Lammas (or Lughnasadh). Wedding day. Start of Celtic autumn. Time for 'gathering in crops'. Look at your commitments, and whether they are joyful.

NEW MOON: A time for going within, new beginnings.

FULL MOON: A time for gratitude and completion. An ideal time for a party!

I celebrate — and have fun!

2

Relationships

1 · OPEN YOUR HEART

MY FRIEND DOROTHY had decided to ask her husband for a divorce, after years of feeling more and more distant from him. He had refused to go for marital counselling, and she felt lonely and sidelined. While he pored over a business report one evening, she worked up the courage to tell him. In desperation, she called upon her soul to help her – and was astounded by what happened next. It was as if reality shifted. Instead of seeing her husband as cold, hostile and rejecting, she suddenly saw a child-like man who was lost, frightened and trying to protect himself. She realised that *she* had judged and rejected *him*. As she gazed at him, she was flooded with the love she had felt for him long ago, when they were young lovers full of hope and dreams. Her anger and neediness melted away, and she no longer felt anxious about the future, knowing that *whatever* happened would be OK.

Instead of asking for a divorce that night, she sat down beside him and said, 'Bill, can we talk? I love you – and I'd almost forgotten that. I feel lost and lonely, and I believe you do too. Is there still enough love left for us to help one another?' He put down his report, and listened to her for the first time in years. They had a long, intimate conversation – and six years on, they are happily married.

When we shift into Soft Time, the fears, doubts and negativity of our ego-self disappear like the morning mist. Instead of seeing the other person from our ego's point of view – 'Look at how he's treating me' / 'She isn't meeting my needs' / 'Is the grass greener elsewhere?' – we see from a higher perspective. We open our heart and know that everyone is holy and innocent, that everyone wants to love and be loved, that hostility and defensiveness are merely masks of our ego-self.

Whenever we speak from our heart rather than our head – when we speak from unconditional love and wisdom – we open ourselves to miracles. Love transforms everything. When Dorothy approached her husband with love, he 'knew' that – for that moment – she was not lost in blame, shame or self-pity, so there was no need to protect himself; and he too responded from love. It was a pivotal moment in their relationship. If Bill had reacted from his ego-self, they would be divorced by now – but he chose to open his heart.

Whatever the problem, in any kind of relationship, opening your heart almost always changes how you approach the situation – and that affects how others respond. Next time you feel stuck or hurt or irritated or outraged, call upon your soul – and ask for your heart to be opened. Wait until you feel a warm glow or tingling in your heart, or a feeling of relaxation and expansion, then look at the situation afresh. When you stop taking it *personally*, and look at it with an open heart, what do you see? What would your heart say in this situation?

Opening your heart also allows us to *listen* – really listen – to the other person. Most of the time, our heads are so full of our *thoughts* about what the other person is saying, or how we feel about it, or what we're going to say next, that we're not really listening at all. Opening your heart means that your thoughts are still, and you feel loving, calm and fully present. *Now* — what is the other person saying?

I open my heart — and listen.

2 · GIVE AND RECEIVE LOVE

MYSTICS HAVE ALWAYS said that love begins and ends with the Self, that we cannot love others unless we first love ourselves. As I understand it, Jesus taught us to 'Love yourself – that you might love others.' (This was twisted by translation into 'Love your neighbour as yourself', which has a very different emphasis.) Many people believe that they will love themselves once someone else loves them *first* – but unless we are a *source* of love, we cannot attract loving relationships.

Unless we love ourselves, we will be anxious and defensive. We will tend to withdraw in social situations, or be over-anxious to please, or needy and dependent, or hide behind a role – thus pushing people away. We might kid ourselves that we have few friends because we live in the city (or country), or because we are poor (or rich), or because we are shy – or that we are happier alone. The truth is that we see ourselves as not good enough and other people as dangerous, and others feel uneasy and guarded in our presence, so our relationships fail to thrive.

Self-love gives us the strength to be vulnerable, to drop our defences, to reveal our own truth – knowing that we have nothing to hide, no need to pretend. As we love and accept ourselves as we are, we become more loving and giving, and genuinely enjoy others' company. Other people feel relaxed and 'safe' with us, and respond by being more open and honest – so we naturally develop good friends and loving relationships.

Self-love means we give love freely, without expecting anything in return – a spontaneous hug, an unexpected bunch of flowers, a warm smile for a stranger, a loving note in a child's lunch box, an offer of help to a friend in need, a cheque to a charity which has touched your heart, or simply saying 'I love you'.

Lack of self-love is why some people are so good at giving, but hopeless at receiving. (Helping professionals often fall into this category.) Unless we are open to receive, we tend to slip into self-pity and martyrhood. Martyrhood often stems from a core belief that suffering and struggle will eventually reap rewards – along with a belief that we don't *deserve* happiness, or must struggle to *earn* love. 'Don't worry about me – you go and have fun!' 'No, I couldn't possibly accept that from you!' 'I have so much to do in so little time.' 'If only I could put my feet up for five minutes!' (Can you hear that martyred sigh?)

Being open to receiving – saying thank you for compliments, accepting gifts graciously, being grateful for the 'magic moments' in everyday life, asking for a hug, welcoming support from others – is a great way to avoid the trap of martyrhood. The martyr within us is secretly angry, and loves to make other people squirm or feel guilty – often without being aware of it – so it is not pleasant to be around; and being a martyr means we rarely relax enough to live in Soft Time.

Whenever we try to give love without being open to receive, our 'love' becomes distorted into something unnatural and unhealthy – such as martyrhood, self-sacrifice, duty, infatuation or obsession. We have blocked the free flow of love. True love always feels good. It makes our heart sing and our spirit dance. It nourishes our soul. But to do this, love has to flow freely – in *both* directions.

I am open to receiving.

3 · REMEMBER THAT THERE IS NO 'OTHER'

WHEN RICHARD CAME to see me, he was full of self-righteous rage because his wife had had an affair. 'I would *never* have done such a thing. I *should* just walk out on her, but I want to know whether our marriage can be saved.' Since he was committed to spiritual growth, I reminded him that the world is a mirror – and that there is no betrayal without self-betrayal. Without condoning his wife's behaviour, I suggested that no one can 'hurt' us unless there is already pain inside, begging for attention.

He looked thoughtful for a while. 'Well, now you mention it – I'm aware that I'm a solicitor because my father wanted me to be one. He dropped out of law school himself, and was determined that I would succeed where he had failed. I did it out of respect for my Dad – but my heart isn't in it. That's how I've betrayed myself, isn't it? I really wanted to do something more creative, like architecture.' And who had his wife had an affair with? You guessed it. It was an architect! She had fallen in love with her husband's 'true self', which he was denying.

It is easier to see other people than to see ourselves, so the Universe helpfully sends us people who mirror what we need to love and accept in ourselves, or who are facing issues which we need to resolve – whether it is our partner, friends, relatives, children, colleagues or clients. Sometimes the most painful lessons are the most transforming, simply because pain is difficult to ignore – and often centres on the very issue we've been busily trying to avoid.

Molly had a destructive relationship with her martyr-ridden and ungrateful mother, who lived 30 miles away but relied heavily upon her daughter for shopping, household tasks and companionship. Since her mother was elderly and diabetic, Molly found it impossible to say no – even when she had to cancel her own arrangements at short notice to meet her mother's constant demands. 'You don't understand', she would say when friends urged her to set some limits. 'My mother's sick – she might die.' Molly believed she was being a loving daughter – but to outsiders, it was obvious that Molly was stuck in martyrhood (like her mother) and that, by giving in to every demand, she was keeping her mother trapped too.

One day, her mother phoned to ask her to 'pop round with a newspaper' – and Molly reached breaking point. She told her mother to go to hell. A few sticky months followed, in which her mother complained and whined and manipulated – but Molly stuck to her guns. She made it clear what she was prepared to do, and where she drew the line – and in time, she and her mother became good friends. Her mother's life blossomed too – as if some soul contract had now been fulfilled, and she no longer had to play her old stuck role.

Seeing the world as a mirror can be a key to understanding and healing our relationships. Each of us is a holographic fragment of All That Is, so whatever we see 'out there' in the world is an aspect of our Self. Whatever qualities we most admire in our heroes and heroines — wisdom, love, courage, creativity, humour, strength — can be found in our own higher Self. And whatever disgusts or enrages us in others is an aspect of our Shadow. (If you ever call your partner your 'other half', you're speaking literally, since couples often 'hold' qualities for each other which the individuals have yet to integrate.) It is almost impossible to be judgemental when we remember that everyone is a mirror!

Everyone I see is part of me.

4 · RESOLVE ANY UNFINISHED BUSINESS

IS THERE ANYONE you need to forgive, or feel guilty about, or never said goodbye to, or long to ask a certain question? *(Just put this book down for a few moments, and see who comes to mind . . . .)* Your emotional body – part of your energy system – is 'holding' this unresolved emotion for you, and is sending a constant trickle of energy to that person, tying you to them and draining your own energy. What is more, we have a natural drive to resolve any unfinished business – so we tend to repeat the same pattern in other relationships, in an attempt to 'get it right' this time. Unfinished business can keep us stuck for years on end – preventing our relationships from working, pushing friends or lovers away, or making us 'act out' in unhelpful ways.

Josephine's mother died when she was three – and none of her relationships, with men or women, had lasted for more than three years. Her emotional body carried the belief that 'Anyone I love leaves me after three years' – and it became a self-fulfilling prophecy. She was 36 years old before she spotted the pattern and began to heal it.

Charlie was sent to boarding school at the age of seven, and had a deep sense of hurt and abandonment. As a child, he believed he was sent away because he was 'bad' – and he later replayed this in his romantic relationships, in which he was loving at first, then became increasingly difficult and hurtful. When he was finally rejected, sometimes after a string of one-night stands, he would triumphantly declare, 'There! I knew she didn't *really* love me!'

One way to resolve unfinished business is to have an inner conversation with the other person. (Whether or not they are still alive, you can connect with anyone at a soul level and they do 'hear' you.) Relax deeply, and imagine you are breathing in love and light – becoming your wise, loving higher Self. Then imagine the other person is standing in front of you, not as their normal personality self, but as their wise loving Self. Say whatever you need to say – speaking from your heart, being totally open and honest, expressing your emotions freely. Listen carefully to any response from the other person. Then notice a dark cord which joins you to the other person, often around the solar plexus. When you are ready, cut this cord – with scissors, a sword or a laser beam – and feel the release of energy. Imagine rubbing a healing ointment into your 'wound' – then say goodbye to the other person, in whatever way feels appropriate.[1]

Forgiveness is often a crucial step in resolving unfinished business. However we cannot forgive someone until we have, first of all, honoured our inner Child's feelings of hurt, rage, sadness or betrayal, and secondly, acknowledged our own role in creating the situation, and what we were hoping to learn from it. Forgiving someone doesn't mean you're letting them off the hook. It means you're letting *yourself* off the hook! It is a gift that we give *ourselves*, so that we free ourselves from the past, and stop giving our energy away to the other person.

We are not victims of our past. The past does not 'cause' us to be hurt, depressed or neurotic in the present. It is our thoughts *right now* which keep the past alive – dwelling on past events, or holding on to dusty old emotions – so that we project the past on to new relationships, and block ourselves from living in the present and reaching for our Dreams. It's one way of staying stuck in Hard Time.

I forgive others – and release the past.

5 · RELEASE YOUR EXPECTATIONS

PERHAPS THE GREATEST source of pain and conflict in relationships is our *expectations* – whether spoken or unspoken – of the other person. It might be a simple and apparently 'reasonable' expectation – I expect my partner to come on holiday with me; I expect my employee to come to work on time; I expect my ten-year-old to keep her bedroom tidy. Or it might be more subtle: expecting someone to be like your mother or father, or to love you unconditionally, or to be your own ideal self, or to heal your childhood, or to fulfil *your* Dreams.

Feeling angry or disappointed in someone invariably means that they have failed to live up to *our* expectations – which raises the question of whether they *should* meet our expectations, rather than simply being who they are. Why shouldn't you or your partner have a solo holiday occasionally? Does your employee really need to come to work at a set time? Should your ten-year-old keep her bedroom tidy just because *you* prefer it? Is there any good reason for these 'rules' – or is it your rigid expectations which are the real problem?

Love means accepting someone just as they are, not as we would like them to be. It means setting them free to follow their own path and be their own person. Sometimes we can resolve relationship difficulties in a moment by releasing our expectations – and apologising, if necessary, for trying to impose our own ideals. (This does not apply, of course, to behaviour which is emotionally or physically abusive, nor when you have *jointly* agreed upon certain rules.)

Whenever you want something from someone that you're not getting – perhaps love, support, honesty, intimacy or commitment – the truth is that you're wanting the other person to fulfil a need which only *you* can fulfil. Perhaps you're not listening to your Dreams and desires, or expecting too much of yourself, or simply not loving and supporting yourself enough? If you wait for the other person to change, you are giving your power away to them. If you instead focus on changing yourself, your relationship will change too; *either* the other person will change, *or* you will end the relationship, *or* their behaviour will no longer trouble you.

Stella consulted me because she was in love with Michael – and was convinced he was her 'one true soulmate'. She thought about him all day long, and clearly idolised him. Michael had shown little interest in her, but she wasn't discouraged by this. She felt sure he was just 'wary of commitment', and seemed to have pinned her hopes for the future on this man. After hearing that I ran workshops on *Attracting a Soulmate*, she came to me for advice.

She looked crestfallen when I told her that metaphysical techniques cannot be used to attract a *specific* person, since this would be manipulation. I also explained that when you're 'in love' with someone from afar, you send a lot of needy energy in their direction, and they pick this up

telepathically and feel pressurised without knowing why –
so you actually push them away at an energy level. I advised
her to get on with her own life, explore why she hadn't
attracted a soulmate up to now and, if she wanted to give
herself a chance with Michael, genuinely set him free and
release any expectations she had about their relationship.
Two years later, she wrote to say that Michael had drifted
out of her life – and she was now happily married to
someone else.

I release my expectations of others.

6 · COMMIT YOURSELF

THE DESIRE FOR intimacy and commitment is almost universal. It stems, firstly, from our longing for Oneness, for perfect love, for overcoming our illusion of separateness; secondly, from knowing that relationships (and parenting) are a major source of growth, and that we cannot learn about love and intimacy by paddling about in the shallow end but must plunge into the depths; and, thirdly, from the fact that it is simply blissful – and such fun – to share our life with someone we love.

The higher purpose of any relationship is learning how to love – and as we get closer to anyone, we inevitably bump into aspects of *ourselves* which make us feel uncomfortable. The 'honeymoon phase' soon passes – with the horrifying realisation that the other person is only human, after all! – and all of our projections and unfinished business come to the surface. At this point, we might feel an urge to run away or convince ourselves that the relationship simply isn't working. Or instead we might say, 'How interesting! What can I learn about myself here?'

When my husband and I first fell in love, he was recently divorced after a long and painful marriage, and I had lived alone most of my adult life – so neither of us had had a loving, intimate relationship. Not surprisingly, we had a lot of 'stuff' to resolve – and it flooded out relentlessly in those early months! All we seemed to do was process our fears, doubts, hurt and anger – and we nearly ended our relationship more than once. We did the classic 'dance of intimacy' in which one person moves closer and feels more loving, and the other responds by pulling away and feeling more distant. However, we knew that our 'stuff' would come up in *any* relationship, and that we must break through our old fears and doubts sometime, with someone – so we agreed to do it as a couple, regardless of whether we then chose to stay together. With this commitment to 'seeing it through' and not taking it all personally, we felt relieved and strangely liberated – and our conflicts began to evaporate. Not long after, we made a lasting commitment to each other.

It takes a lot of psychic energy to search for a partner, and it can be a huge relief to say 'My search is over – I will commit myself to *this* person.' Commitment frees up psychic energy, and makes it much easier to live in Soft Time. (Just before John and I decided to marry, the exhaust dropped off my car. I was literally 'exhausted' by our indecision over commitment!)

Of course, commitment feels scary unless we are first committed to 'be there' for *ourselves*. Since our relationships with others mirror our relationship with ourselves, being our own best friend has to come before any meaningful commitment to another. We meet the 'right person' when we *are* the 'right person'.

Commitment to someone else isn't necessarily right for everyone, but it can be a spiritual journey in itself: an infinite process of discovery, an enthralling adventure, a shared joy, a sacrament. It means loving and being loved. It means sharing your lives, devoting time and energy to being together, nurturing each other, being open and honest, actively listening to one another and working through any issues between you. It means supporting each other's Dreams and visions, having fun together and giving each other the space to 'be'.

Happily our relationships become easier and more relaxed as we shift into Soft Time, since we are no longer ruled by fear. As natural mystics, our relationships are based upon a shared commitment to personal and spiritual growth, being willing to discover Self through a relationship with the Other – and having fun together.

I commit myself to being my own best friend.

7 · See Conflict as a Source of Growth

WHENEVER TWO PEOPLE come together – as friends, colleagues or lovers – they are often 'on their best behaviour' for a while, avoiding any possible conflicts, agreeing readily and often pretending to be more alike than they really are. As they relax and feel more confident with each other, their differences slowly emerge – and they might seem less compatible than before. For someone who lacks self-confidence, this can feel quite threatening and they might try to hide or minimise their differences. But sooner or later, their deep Self will urge them to do or say something which leads to conflict and disagreement.

Conflict can be a wonderful source of growth and change. It is 'grist for the mill'. (Whenever I hear of a couple who 'haven't had an argument in 20 years', I wonder whether they have grown at all during that time!) By clarifying how we are different from others, we discover more about who we are, and deepen our relationships by being more honest with each other. We also learn how to take care of our own needs, and how to handle emotions in positive ways.

Resolving conflict does not mean reaching a compromise. (Compromise tends to mean agreeing half-heartedly on something that suits neither party.) Resolution means finding a higher 'win-win' solution that works well for both of you.

Sometimes this means taking the focus off trying to change the other person, and looking at how you need to change yourself – perhaps through lifestyle changes, or processing your beliefs, or responding to old behaviour in a new way. If one person in a relationship changes, the other *has* to shift in some way – so if you've been waiting for the other person to 'sort themselves out', this is a good way of taking your power back while also changing the relationship.

Another way to resolve conflicts is to focus on what is working well. Instead of complaining that your friends always wait for *you* to phone, be grateful for the fact that they're always delighted to hear from you. We attract what we focus on – so focusing on what is positive can 'magically' resolve other issues.

It is essential to steer clear of blame-and-shame tactics. As soon as you believe the other person is at fault, or needs to change, or is 'making' you miserable, you'll get lost in hurt, resentment or self-pity *and* put them on the defensive – so the problem tends to escalate. Likewise, if you assume that *you're* in the wrong, your feelings of shame, guilt or self-doubt will cut you off from your higher wisdom. If you assume you're both doing your best, and no one is to blame, it makes it far easier to resolve any conflicts.

Of course, conflict is only *one* possible source of growth in relationships. If you see it as the only – or best – way to learn and grow, you'll feel uneasy whenever a relationship is going well! We also grow together through intimacy and sharing, loving and caring, relaxing together and supporting each other's Dreams. But it helps us approach conflict in a positive way if we see it as a pointer towards growth, rather than as a sign that anything is 'wrong': 'What is the opportunity here? What can I learn about myself? How can we work this out together?'

I am willing to be different.

8 · ALWAYS RESERVE JUDGEMENT

IF YOU HEAR about a child being assaulted, a house being burgled, hostages being taken or a bomb exploding in a busy street, what is your usual reaction? Do you immediately blame and judge those involved? Or do you mentally send love and light to them all – knowing that they are human beings, just like you?

Most of us leap straight in with our judgements: 'How could anyone do that . . ?' 'That is really sick!' 'How could they be so heartless?' Our ego-self is always eager to judge, eager to blame, eager to be right where others are wrong. When there is a problem, our ego-self wants to know who is responsible. It loves to make comparisons, and wants to feel 'better than' others – so it can be moralistic and intolerant.

The Seneca wisdom of North America says that whenever we point a finger in blame, three fingers point back at us. (Watch your hand when it points – it is true.) Other mystery traditions also suggest that what we give out returns three times over – so it makes good sense to send out unconditional love rather than judgement.

It isn't always easy to reserve judgement. If someone behaves badly towards us or (even trickier) towards someone we love, it is tempting to see them as bad, stupid or ignorant, to vent our anger, to curse them; but this means we *separate* ourselves from them, and shift automatically into Hard Time. Instead we might refuse to take it personally, and assume that the person must be hurt, angry or frightened in order to behave in that way – and that *we* might behave that way in similar circumstances. We can mentally send love and acceptance to the person instead of anger and hostility and, without judging ourselves, ask how and why we attracted that situation. This way, we learn from the experience *and* remain in the pure bliss of Soft Time. Always reserving judgement is a good recipe for inner peace.

One way to reserve judgement is to remind ourselves that we can never see the whole picture. If a stranger honks their horn angrily at us, we cannot know what stresses they might be facing that day – we have not 'walked a mile in the other's shoes' – so it is wise to send them good wishes, and let it go. If someone is begging on the street, we cannot know their life story or their higher purpose; if we did, we might feel compassion and perhaps admiration for them. If someone has murdered a child, we have not witnessed their own childhood, or lived with their disturbed thoughts and feelings; we do not know what suffering they have seen – or we might feel pity even for them. 'There but for the grace of God go I . . . .'

Similarly, we can reserve judgement on God/Goddess for creating a world that has seen so much suffering. We do not see the full picture – so let's not assume that God is either powerless or uncaring. If we were aware of the whole story, we would perhaps understand.

Reserving judgement doesn't mean being indifferent to what happens. It is human and appropriate to feel outraged when we seem to be mistreated, or when we hear of unnecessary suffering. However, we can choose to stand aside from blaming or judging those involved, send love and light – and move on from there. If we are slow to blame or judge others, *all* of our relationships will be more loving and harmonious – and we will be easy on ourselves too.

I trust that everyone is doing the best they can.

9 · BE WILLING TO LET GO

MARRIAGE OFTEN ENDS in divorce these days – and old friends might part after many years – not because you have 'failed', but because the rapid rate of growth and change means that you're more likely to *outgrow* a relationship before one of you dies, especially if you were very young when you met. Perhaps you've grown in different directions and are no longer compatible, or perhaps you have completed the task for which you came together (such as to have or raise children, help each other towards independence, to release martyrhood or find inner security).

Commitment does not mean being 'stuck' in a relationship, come what may. It does mean being *very reluctant* to end it, until you feel sure in your heart that there is little alternative, that it is the right decision and that you're not just 'running away'. But if a relationship consistently drains your energy and no longer serves your growth, then it is probably time to let go.

Some people tend to be *over*-committed, and cling to a relationship long after others would have said goodbye – perhaps from a misguided sense of duty or loyalty, or from anxiety about being alone, or because they have projected some of their Self on to their partner which they need to reclaim. (Look at the qualities – good *and* bad – you see in your partner, and be willing to embrace your 'other half'. This makes it much easier to let go of the relationship.)

If your partner is violent, abusive or compulsively unfaithful, then commitment is inappropriate and self-abusive. It is time to leave *now* – *then* ask questions about how you created that situation, and how to avoid it in future. (How come your self-esteem is so low? In what way are you abusing yourself? How might you love yourself more?) Don't waste time analysing *why* your partner was abusive, and how you might help him (or her)! That is one of the traps of co-dependency, which keeps us stuck in Hard Time. Get out – and learn to take care of yourself.

In other cases, it is less clear whether it is time to end a relationship. Perhaps you don't have enough in common to be friends or lovers any more. Perhaps you have drifted along together for years, companionably but without real intimacy – and you feel bored and restless. Perhaps you feel more and more frustrated because your partner resists growth, or discourages you from making changes. Perhaps you have both grown up over the years, but your relationship has remained stuck. Or perhaps you simply cannot talk to each other about anything emotional or meaningful, and your 'issues' remain unresolved for years on end.

If you are the one who is most willing to grow and change, it is likely to be you who wants to end the relationship. Your friend or partner might resist, telling you they couldn't cope without you, or that you're being selfish or disloyal – perhaps mirroring your own fear and resistance. This is the time to remember the spiritual law about relationships: *Whatever is right for you is right for the other person* (even if they protest strongly at a personality level). If a relationship isn't working for you, it isn't working for the other person either – and if you cannot resolve the problem, it is time to move on.

If so, the challenge is to release each other *with love*. There might be sadness, yes, since grief is a healthy part of the process of letting go. But ideally there will be no blame, no guilt, no regret, no recriminations. Just letting go with love – and blessing each other as you go your separate ways.

I am willing to let go – if the time is right.

10 · LIVE YOUR OWN LIFE

DO YOU TEND to 'disappear' in relationships? Are you a compulsive carer, who focuses on others' needs at the expense of your own? Do you attract 'lame dogs'? Do you *need* to be in a relationship? Do you worry constantly about how you look, or what others think of you? Perhaps you feel more comfortable with children (or clients) than with an equal partner? Or see commitment as a prison? Do you avoid intimate relationships, and bury yourself in busyness? Are you addicted to drugs, alcohol, smoking, work, exercise, shopping – or anything else? If the answer is Yes to any of these, you probably have a problem with codependency.

In a classic codependent relationship, there often *seems* to be one supportive, competent person and one more needy, dependent, child-like person – though these roles might sometimes swap around. (A famous example was the marriage of the Prince and Princess of Wales.) The two people might be husband and wife, parent and child, friends, relatives or neighbours; or it might be a professional relationship – boss and worker, therapist and client, or charity worker and recipient.

Codependency involves keeping others at a distance, either by appearing competent, cheerful and in control, *or* by pretending to be weak, passive and helpless – thus avoiding true intimacy. A hallmark of codependency is *inequality*. It traps people in complementary roles which prevent them from growing and changing. The subconscious contract in such relationships is that the 'weak' partner will be taken care of, instead of growing up and taking responsibility for themselves, while the 'strong' partner gets to feel valued, indispensable or even heroic, and can deny their own neediness, dependence and low self-esteem. (Other codependents are obsessed with relationships which are pure fantasy, or unlikely to last, or which ended many years ago, to protect themselves from true intimacy.)

Codependency means that your primary focus is *outside* the Self – that you seek happiness or self-esteem in the outside world, instead of going within. Over the years, this can become an increasingly desperate search which – apart from blocking personal intimacy – leads to workaholism, alcoholism, shopaholism, eating disorders and other addictions. It is hugely widespread in our culture, but is often disguised in socially acceptable forms such as being 'caring', 'committed' or 'independent' – or is hidden away in the dark corners of our private lives.

To move beyond codependency, it is essential to live your *own* life – not someone else's. This means focusing less on others and the world, and directing more of your energy *inwards*, so that you get to know yourself well. It means getting clear about your boundaries – *your* beliefs, *your* Dreams, *your* needs, *your* feelings, *your* limits, *your* inner guidance – and saying No whenever appropriate. It also means making time and space for yourself. Yes, even if you have small children *and* a partner *and* a demanding job! You might create a sanctuary where you spend a quiet half-hour each day, or go on retreat occasionally or – like me – have a weekly Time-For-Me slot when you do whatever you fancy. (Depending on the weather, I go for a long walk – often with my camera and lenses – or do some abstract painting.)

In the short-term, our loved ones might protest when we grow and change, and assert our own needs – but in the long-term, it *protects* our close relationships, and relieves our fear of intimacy and commitment. It allows us to re-centre ourselves and express our deep Self – so we can offer our wholeness to others.

I am at the centre of my own life. I honour my own needs.

3

Parenting

1 · CHERISH THE MAGIC MOMENTS

PARENTING IS FULL of magic moments: a child's first steps, kicking autumn leaves together, building a snowman, watching seedlings grow, a spontaneous hug, exploring rock pools or building a treehouse . . . . Yet how often have you heard parents say, 'I'm looking forward to my child walking/being out of nappies/going to school/being more independent/leaving home.' Many parents are forever rushing their children on to the next stage, and the next – never enjoying *this* stage, this week, this moment. Others look back wistfully on their children's early years, while moaning about how difficult their kids are *now*.

Childhood is so precious and ephemeral, yet many children grow up while their parents are rushing about doing other things, or resenting and complaining about them. (Grandparents often *enjoy* children more than their parents do, because they are less hurried and task-focused. They appreciate the magic of the moment.)

Even ordinary moments can be full of magic. With a young child, cleaning, cooking or washing with their 'help' makes a routine task into a shared experience. Yes, it might be slower and messier – but how much more fun! (The child is learning and happy – and you don't have to worry about keeping them occupied while you get the job done.) At the age of two, Kieran often helps me in the office by licking stamps or unpacking boxes – and is becoming expert at emptying the dishwasher, putting clothes into the tumble dryer and tidying up his toys. If ever I feel impatient and want to get on with a task, I remind myself that he's helping me live in Soft Time – so I take a deep breath, relax and enjoy the slower pace of life. I've also noticed again and again that he tends to whine and pull at me when I am preoccupied and *not present*, relaxing and settling as soon as I bring myself back into the moment.

Cherishing the magic moments of parenting means being aware of the bigger picture – the breathtaking miracle of childbirth, the awesome gift of being a parent, the joy of sharing your life with a child, the wonder at your children's constant learning and development. It means knowing that their childhood will pass all too quickly – and that every single day is to be treasured.

Few children will cherish memories of video games or watching TV as they get older. It is more likely their hearts will swell as they recall that glorious sunny day when they built a dam across a stream, picked blackberries from the hedgerow and scrambled over rocky crags, or the night they camped beside the ocean and watched the sun rise. (Think back to fond memories from your own childhood.[1]) Yet most children devote the majority of their leisure time to staring at a small screen.

Part of our responsibility as parents is to make sure our children have a plentiful store of magic memories – relaxed Soft-Time days drenched with joy and laughter – so that they grow up loving life, and feeling valued and appreciated. It helps to ensure that we enjoy their childhood too, rather than merely 'getting through' it!

If you're cleaning the kitchen floor for the second time this week while your children beg you to play in the garden or help with a jigsaw – 'Not now, I'm busy!' – what message does this give them about your priorities? As you fall asleep tonight, would you rather look back on mopping the floor yet again, or laughing with your children as you catch a ball in the garden, or tackle that jigsaw together?

I see the magic in every moment.

2 · BE A POSITIVE PARENT

I ATTENDED A playgroup once – just once! – where a small gathering of stressed-out mothers huddled around a low table to complain non-stop about how tiring, difficult, noisy, messy and generally impossible their children were. I made one or two comments about how grateful I felt to be a parent, and how much fun it was – but I was simply frowned at. I quickly retreated to play with the toddlers.

Complaining about children is a cultural pastime, rather like whinging about the weather. It can become a way of fitting in, of 'belonging' to a group – and like anything else, it becomes a self-fulfilling prophecy. If you keep telling your kids they are bad or stupid or clumsy or untidy, they'll do their best to live up to your image of them. Likewise if we genuinely enjoy our children's company, they will grow up believing they are pleasant and interesting to be with – and so they will be.

The 'problem' with children does not lie in children – who are wise, loving, wonderful beings of Light. The problem lies in our Hard Time attitudes towards parenting. If we see children as hard work or a burden, constantly struggle to 'stay on top' of the chaos, moan about the noise and try to control our children, parenting will be a highly stressful and negative experience. Choosing a more positive attitude towards parenting – or recognising that our lifestyle is too stressful and has to change – could transform our daily life.

When we're in Hard Time, for example, young children making a mess is seen as a problem, a chore, an additional task, more busyness. In Soft Time, all parenting is seen as sacred work. We are always aware of the bigger picture. A 'mess' becomes a sign of a child's exploration, learning and ability to have impact on the world. We might dash to catch the falling milk carton, but we are also filled with wonder at our child's evolving skills and fascination with the world. Yes, the mess needs clearing up – but unless life is over-busy and tightly scheduled, mess-clearing is not a problem. It is an everyday part of loving our children.

When my elder stepson was 13, he was moody, depressive and laconic – and I'm ashamed to say that I saw it as part of 'him', and found him difficult to be with. By the time he was 16, now a delightful young man, his younger brother had become moody, sullen and negative. (His elder brother said to us at the time, 'I apologise for having been 13 once!') Having been through this before, my husband and I could 'see the bigger picture' and recognise that the chatty, caring and humorous boy we used to know would eventually re-emerge in a more mature form. By seeing his moodiness as a phase – a response to adolescent hormones and social pressures – we were able to take a much more positive attitude.

Many years ago, I counselled the mother of a teenager who had leukaemia. She recalled how she had often shouted at him for leaving his room untidy or dishes unwashed. She swore that, if he recovered, she would stop fretting about trivia and be more loving and grateful for having a child at all.

We can choose to focus on the thousand-and-one ways in which parenting is stressful, chaotic and demanding – or we can focus on the love, joy, wonder and delight of being a parent. As one writer puts it, 'The hard truth is that if you aren't enjoying your parenting, your child isn't enjoying being a child.'[2]

I revel in the magic of parenting.

3 · HEAL YOUR OWN INNER CHILD

EVERYONE HAS 'WOUNDS' from their childhood. Whether you suffered abuse as a child, or lost one or both parents, or simply went through the 'normal' traumas of growing up in a family, your inner Child is sure to carry some emotional scars. Even if you had a stable background with loving parents, it is unlikely you were always given unconditional love and respect. After all, parents are only human.

When I worked as a psychotherapist, I was struck by how often family patterns were passed down the generations – not only violence and abuse, but also more subtle patterns which the child was often unaware of. One client had had a child at the age of 16, with a much older boyfriend who had immediately abandoned her. She had given the child up for adoption – and *later* discovered not only that her mother had been through the same experience at the same age, but also her grandmother. Another client's father died when she was 11. Her mother remarried two years later, and her new stepfather sexually abused her. Years later, her mother revealed that this was a repetition of her own childhood.

It seems that unless we deal with the emotional wounds of our own childhood, we pass them on to our children – perhaps hoping they will heal and release the pattern *for* us.

(Or we might simply do the opposite – being laissez-faire if our parents were overcontrolling, and so on.) Children often act out our own unresolved conflicts – so if you had a difficult adolescence, so might your child; if you're neurotic about food and weight, your child might be even more so. They also absorb our way of dealing with emotions, handling relationships and approaching life in general.

Part of our responsibility as parents is to heal our own inner Child, so that our wounds are *not* passed down the generations. Healing ourselves is a way of protecting our own children, while also playing an important part in the healing of future generations. (It also makes parenting easier, since children tend to 'act out' or develop problems when there are unresolved conflicts within the family.)

Of course, one reason why we choose to have children is because they can *help* us to heal our inner Child. When a father buys a train-set for his three-month-old baby, it is his own inner Child who has nudged him into the purchase! Playing and having fun with our children is a simple but effective way of healing ourselves.

Another approach to healing your inner Child is to meet him or her on an inner journey. Imagine yourself in your childhood home, all alone – and search for your inner Child. You might find your Child in your bedroom, in a 'safe place' where you used to hide, or in the garden or back yard. Introduce yourself as their grown-up self, and say you have come to be their friend. Then sit down and *listen*. Your inner Child might be shy or wary at first, or over-eager to please – but eventually he or she will begin to talk about their concerns: perhaps reminding you of long-forgotten events, or raging at you for ignoring them for so long, or sobbing uncontrollably about a loss or other painful memory, or complaining that you never have *fun* any more. *Just listening* – and perhaps hugging your inner Child as it unburdens itself – is a huge step in the healing process.

I am committed to my own inner Child.

4 · Parent from Your Deep Self

Parenting is a course in love, and a thrilling journey of self-discovery. It is a heavenly opportunity to practise unconditional love, and learn the true meaning of Oneness. However, many of us approach parenthood in a dualistic way – seeing parenting as a battleground between ego-selves, or seeing children as 'lesser beings' who need to be shaped and moulded into proper human beings. (Many popular parenting books reflect this need to control and manipulate our children – a need based on fear and separation.) This is the basis of all forms of child abuse – from milder forms such as 'controlled crying' (that is, teaching your baby that you won't respond to their distress, so that they learn to keep quiet) or threats ('Do that again and you'll be sorry') through to blatant emotional, physical or sexual abuse.

Parenting is full of conflict when we're stuck in our ego-selves, seeing ourselves as separate from our children. When we are living in Hard Time, our ego-self can feel threatened by our child and want to 'protect' itself, its time, its energy, its home, its space. Certainly no one can be prepared for the extent to which a child 'takes over' your life – but the ego-self is often unwilling to *surrender* to parenting, and to sharing one's life with a child in a loving and respectful way.

When we're in Soft Time we know that, at a deep level, parent and child are One. We bask in the everyday wonder of this mystical experience called parenthood; and we see that our child is holy, innocent, loving – whatever their surface behaviour. We tackle any challenge not by obeying others' rules or following 'expert' advice, but by listening to our own inner voice of Love. The true magic of parenting comes from tapping into this wellspring of 'boundless love'[3] and Oneness.

Every event in our lives – whether changing a nappy, washing dishes or watching the sun set – can be experienced at these two different levels. At the level of surface reality, life tends to seem chaotic, fragmented and meaningless. If this is all we experience, it is no wonder if parenting (and life itself) feels stressful and draining. However, the deeper level of love and Oneness can be experienced whenever we are living in Soft Time. At this level, we see the bigger picture – and *experience* the underlying unity, harmony, order and meaningfulness of everything. Even changing a nappy becomes an experience of love, tenderness, intimacy and (often) laughter.

I know from my own experience that we can shift rapidly from one level to the other. When Kieran tipped a carton of washing powder over the kitchen carpet recently, I initially reacted from my ego-self with irritation and frustration, and grabbed the carton too roughly from his hands. I immediately caught myself. I took a deep breath and 'saw' the situation from my deep Self. I laughed and hugged my precious son – 'You little rascal!' – who giggled and hugged my neck; then I cheerfully cleared up the mess, feeling nothing but love and gratitude.

Boundless love means allowing our children to be who they are – which means loving them even when they're making a mess, throwing a tantrum, being sullen or sarcastic, trailing in the egg-and-spoon race or failing their exams. When we parent from our deep Self instead of from our ego, we shift our whole approach to parenting. Instead of being an endless series of tasks, a source of frustration and exhaustion, or an opportunity for pride (or shame), parenting becomes a cherished opportunity – to be with another human being as they unfold in the arms of Love.

I see my child through the eyes of Love.

5 · HONOUR YOUR CHILDREN AS TEACHERS

IF WE GET lost in the practicalities of parenting, we can easily miss the point. Parenting is essentially a *relationship*, not a set of tasks and activities. What is more, it is a *two-way* relationship. Children are equal but different – and teach us at least as much as we teach them, at many different levels.

If you believe that children come into existence at the moment of conception or birth (or somewhere in between), you might be forgiven for believing that parents are supposed to teach their children, but not vice versa. But my belief is that children arrive with their own personality, issues and chosen destiny – and that they are often older and wiser souls than their parents, who have come as our teachers. Your children have probably been your mother or father in a past life, your spiritual teacher, colleague and friend – and might sometimes feel frustrated at being treated 'like a child'.

(If you doubt whether we have lived before, you might have to set aside any religious teachings from childhood, and consult your deep Self. I have no doubt, for example, that Jesus taught reincarnation. It was only in the 6th century AD that reincarnation was removed from the Bible – for purely political reasons.)[4]

Between the ages of three and seven, many children have what I call a 'window of wisdom', in which they speak readily from their deep Self, often with remarkable clarity and insight. I've heard dozens of examples of young children telling their parents that they 'chose' them, and why; or pronouncing with great authority on the nature of God, the existence of angels or the meaning and purpose of life. A mother wrote to me about her four-year-old, who had declared in the midst of an argument: 'Mummy, you *know* the only reality is love!' (Needless to say, her precocious statement ended their argument!) Other children talk about their past lives, often using concepts and vocabulary beyond their years.[5]

It is important for us to listen respectfully, rather than laughing or dismissing such statements. Young children 'know' that the world is full of magic and miracles, and often have striking psychic abilities – yet sadly, most children are taught that such ideas are false and 'childish', and gradually learn to ignore their deep Self.

Children not only teach us by what they say – but even more, by how they are. ('Unless you become like little children, you will not enter the kingdom of heaven . . .') When we are very young, we are embodied mystics who dwell naturally in the pure bliss of Soft Time. Watch a young child playing, and you will marvel at their total absorption, their ability to live in the moment, their joy and laughter, their spontaneity and creativity, their exuberance and delight in the natural world. Children don't need a reason to be happy; they are simply glad to be alive.

There are countless other lessons to learn from children – such as learning to accept change and take life as it comes;

becoming more patient; dealing with emotion in a healthy way; or being relatively ego-less (which children are until their teenage years!) A useful question to ask yourself is: 'If this child is my teacher, what lessons am I supposed to learn?'

I am willing to learn from my child(ren).

6 · NOURISH YOUR CHILD'S CONSCIOUSNESS

I RECENTLY BOUGHT a 'Peter Rabbit' video for my toddler, believing it to be a heartwarming tale. (After all, I grew up with the stories of Beatrix Potter.) I was shocked to find that the story featured a horrifying man who threatened to put the long-eared little hero in a pie, and – even worse – showed two frightened young rabbits being beaten with a cane by an adult rabbit! Needless to say, the video promptly disappeared from our shelf – but it made me wonder about the messages we unknowingly give our children. The destructive messages of Hard Time – such as 'The world is a dangerous place', 'You have to be "good" to stay safe', 'Life is one problem after another' and 'It's a struggle to survive' – seem to be all too common, even in stories aimed at very young children.

Children are like sponges. They greedily absorb the beliefs, attitudes and emotional states around them, eager to learn about the world they live in. In the early years, they have no way of questioning what they see, hear and feel. They simply take it in. As parents, we have a responsibility to nourish our children's consciousness – not to wrap them in cotton wool but to ensure that, as far as possible, they inhabit the carefree, loving and creative world of Soft Time.

Fear and criticism can creep into so much that we say to our children – from correcting their early language ('No, it's not a dog. It's a cat.') and even their play ('No, you're meant to build a tower with these, not pour water into them!') to filling them with dire warnings of impending catastrophe ('Be careful! You'll fall!', 'Don't run into the road – you'll get run over!', 'If you fail your exams, you'll never get a decent job!') Every parent is doing the very best they can, but most of us repeat what our own parents said to us – and their parents said to them – often without really listening to ourselves.

If we give our children images of failure and disaster, they might become over-anxious and unsure of themselves, or reckless and accident-prone. It only takes a little extra thought to express what we need to say in a positive way – to give helpful information rather than anxiety-laden warnings. ('Yes, it's *like* a dog isn't it? It's a cat.' 'Hold on tight and you'll stay safe.' 'Cross the road carefully and you'll be fine.' 'If you pass your exams, it will be easier to get the job you want.') If you're tense while speaking to your child, your child will get anxious too – and you'll soon be in a vicious circle of increasing stress and tension; whereas if you're relaxed and heart-centred, your child will relax too – and you stay in Soft Time.

Children of this generation need to know *about* Hard Time, without living *in* it – like mystics through the ages who have been 'in the world but not of it'. This means surrounding them with love, joy, laughter, freedom, beauty, harmony and nature; encouraging imagination and creativity; and probably limiting TV-watching, since TV mostly reflects the fear, struggle, victimhood, melodrama and materialism of Hard Time, and it *is* addictive. (The average child watches TV for three hours per day; that's 17,500 hours or *two years* of childhood staring at a flickering screen!)

It also means living in Soft Time ourselves, and nourishing our *own* consciousness – since even more than what we do or say, children absorb *what is going on inside us*. (If you are secretly terrified that your child will take drugs, they will be far more intrigued than if you simply trust that drugs will be of no interest to them.) If *we* live in Soft Time, our children will grow up experiencing Soft Time as 'normal', and Hard Time as an aberration – instead of the other way around.

I surround my child(ren) with love, joy and creativity.

7 · Avoid Shame, Blame and Praise

A HEALTHY CHILD grows up feeling good about themselves, and being motivated by *intrinsic reward*: that is, choosing any activity for the sheer joy or challenge of it – rather than for approval or reward, or as a way of rebelling or opting-out.

Unfortunately parents (and teachers) can damage a child's self-esteem by using shame-and-blame tactics: 'Can't you do *anything* right?' 'You were trouble from the moment you were born', 'Why can't you be more like your sister?', 'Can't you shut up?', 'Don't be an idiot!' If you believe that children are basically antisocial or just plain bad – and so need to be controlled and 'civilised' – then criticising them might be a misguided attempt to knock them into shape 'for their own good'.

If, on the other hand, you view children as wondrous beings of Light who are naturally loving and social, you will assume that any undesirable behaviour is a *mistake*, which stems from lack of information, lack of skill or misunderstanding – or from a genuine clash between the adult's and the child's (equally valid) needs. (Often children just need a clearly formulated rule – such as 'You're not allowed to take a toy out of someone else's hand' – in order to behave impeccably.)

A poor school report might lead a shame-and-blame parent to exclaim, 'What's the meaning of this? You'll stay in every night until your results get better, you lazy good-for-nothing!' Such a child will not only shrink in shame, and find it difficult to give of their best – but will also feel misunderstood and unloved. A parent who lives in Soft Time, on the other hand, might read the same report and gently ask their child, 'How do you feel about this report? Yes, I thought perhaps you were disappointed. What do you think is going wrong?' – followed by a heart-to-heart discussion which leaves the child feeling both valued and optimistic.

The dangers of shaming-and-blaming children are fairly obvious if we give it a moment's thought – but it might seem odd to suggest that we shouldn't *praise* children. Doesn't praise make us feel good about ourselves? Not necessarily. Firstly, a positive label can promote the ego-self, and be almost as damaging and limiting as a negative label. 'You're such a good girl' is a judgement based upon *pleasing others*, and meeting others' expectations – which might encourage her to be a doormat, people-pleaser, martyr or compulsive helper in adult life. Not necessarily what is intended! In the same way, 'Clever boy!' might really mean 'You make *me* feel proud' – and puts pressure on a child to perform. Secondly, if we always praise or reward a child for good performance, they come to expect and need this – like the child who shows their report card *in order* to get extra pocket money, or who cannot get on with a task unless someone else is watching.

Young children are eager to learn *for its own sake*, rather than to please their parents, or gain a gold star – and the wrong kind of praise can disrupt this natural love of learning. If a child becomes more interested in showing a drawing to its parents than in actually doing the drawing, its motivation is moving outside its Self.

So how can we praise children in a way that supports their growth? One useful guideline is to *label the activity, not the child* – e.g. 'I bet you're really pleased with this drawing!' or 'That's getting easier and easier for you, isn't it?' or 'You've made a lovely job of sweeping the floor' – rather than 'Gosh, aren't you clever!' or 'You *are* a helpful girl/boy!' Also, *share how you feel* rather than judging what they've done – e.g. 'I love your giggle! It makes me feel happy', 'I'm so glad that you're pleased with your school report', 'I really appreciate your help'.

I support my child(ren)'s sense of self-worth.

8 · VALUE SILENCE, STILLNESS AND SOLITUDE

As A CHILD, I spent countless happy hours meandering along the nearby beach and promenade, gazing out to sea, exploring woods and streams, playing with my rabbit, wondering at the stars – or reading books, writing stories and poems, or just sitting and pondering in my bedroom. Although I had two brothers to play with, I also loved to spend time alone – time to think, time to be.

I recently spent time with a family with children aged nine and 12 whose lives were a whirlwind of programmed activities – all day at school (with its strict timetable), then after-school clubs and sports, home for dinner, then off to a music teacher, play rehearsal or dance class before flopping in front of the TV until bedtime. There was no *space* in their lives! The children's energy was all focused on the outer world, and they looked to others for direction. If they had a moment to spare, they seemed anxious to fill it – usually by flicking on the TV. They were privileged children in so many ways – with loving parents and a beautiful home – yet they seemed hyped up, tense and out of balance. I did not envy them their frantically busy and demanding childhood.

Parents often believe it is required of them to organise their children's every moment – take them to amusement parks, buy the latest toys and play-stations, provide a taxi service to countless clubs and classes – in the belief that this 'stimulating' environment will boost their child's potential. (Presumably this is based on the idea that babies and children are empty vessels which need to be filled.) The result is that children grow up passive, easily bored, expecting to be entertained, living vicariously through the TV and media stars. They lose touch with their own inner resources, and become alienated from the natural world.

A child who is always busy and entertained might have a 'rich environment' – but will grow up infinitely poorer than a child who is encouraged to value stillness, silence and solitude. A busy child will grow up learning to live in Hard Time; whereas a child who is allowed plenty of space for unstructured play and 'timeless time', with periods of solitude and privacy – no chatting, no TV or radio, no computer, no expectations – is likely to retain the ability to go within, to listen to their inner wisdom, to pay attention to their feelings, to be creative, to have a sense of awe and wonder, to feel whole and complete, to feel at One.

Children who are more introvert will find it comes more naturally – but *all* children (and adults!) need time to gaze into space, to daydream, to potter and dawdle, to sit and 'do nothing'. It is crucial to retaining their natural state of enlightenment, of awareness, of joy in simply being alive. Yet how often are children told to 'Stop daydreaming' or 'Don't just sit there, *do* something!' by stressed adults who have forgotten how to be simple and joyful.

A few practical suggestions:

- Have a family 'quiet evening' once a week – no TV, no

computer, no visitors, no phone calls.

- Meditate together. Children as young as three can learn to sit quietly for a few minutes – and slip away when they have had enough.
- Make sure *everyone* gets time and space to themselves – even if the space is temporary (e.g. 'I'm using the guest room/bathroom/dining room for the next hour').
- Encourage your children to potter, daydream and 'do nothing'. Beyond boredom lies the deep Self.

Silence, stillness and solitude are precious.

9 · BE A GOOD ROLE MODEL

SEVERAL TIMES, I'VE heard a parent *shouting* at a child to be *quiet* – and even *slap* their child for *hitting* another child! This is rather like trying to force peace by dropping bombs! It is unreasonable to expect a child to be more adult than we are. (If *we* feel the need to shout or hit, why shouldn't they?) Children learn much of their behaviour from us. A loud or aggressive child will often have a loud or aggressive parent. If a child never seems to listen, does anyone really listen to them? If they seem selfish, does anyone consider *their* needs and wishes enough, or bother to find out how they feel and what they really want?

It is crucial to be good role models for children. Young children see their parents as gods – perfect, beyond reproach – which is why they either blame themselves if parents behave badly, or assume it is 'normal' behaviour and copy it.

Parents can provide good examples of how to be loving adults. Our ego-self often defines love as self-sacrifice or martyrhood (giving up your life for your children), or as 'worrying' about your children – in other words, sending them negative energy ('I only worry because I care about you!'). This is not what Love is all about! We cannot truly love our children unless we love and nurture ourselves too; and instead of sending them fear and anxiety, we need to hold *visions* for their future. By being loving, creative and joyful people who live a balanced lifestyle, fulfil our Dreams *and* enjoy our children – or at least are heading in that direction! – we provide a positive role model for both parenting *and* adulthood.

It is also important to allow ourselves to be human. It isn't necessary to wear a halo, or struggle to be the 'perfect parent'. If we are hard on ourselves, we teach our children to be self-critical too, which increases their anxiety and damages their self-esteem – so part of being a good role model is being gentle and loving with ourselves, and allowing ourselves to be 'good enough' as parents.

If you lose your temper with your child, for example, it isn't the end of the world. Just acknowledge it, and step out of the situation if necessary while you calm down. Then apologise to your child and explain what happened – taking responsibility for your emotions, rather than blaming your child: 'I'm sorry I shouted at you. I'm very tired today, so I'm easily upset.' Don't pretend you're not angry, or you'll confuse them and make them doubt their intuitions. (If you find yourself actually *hitting* or shaking your child in anger, then get professional help fast.)

It is equally important to allow our *children* to be human. Most of us have an ideal image of how we would like our children to be – which might reflect our own 'ideal self', or what our ego-self thinks would make *us* look good in the eyes of others. Or – more positively – it might be an image based upon what we intuitively sense to be our child's potential. However, if you expect your child to live up to this ideal image, they might rebel and become the opposite – or try hard to please you but always feel that they have disappointed you, and be unsure of who they really are.

Children need to feel loved for being who they are, with all their warts and imperfections. No one should be expected to be a saint – child *or* parent – or to be clever or successful or funny or wise or happy or energetic or beautiful or caring *all* of the time. It is OK to have a crumpled shirt or untied shoelaces, to have knobbly knees or pimples, to be shy or grumpy or negative, or slump in an exhausted heap from time to time. It is more than OK to be human!

I am a loving role model for my child(ren).

10 · ENCOURAGE YOUR CHILD TO MAKE ACTIVE CHOICES

SINCE PARENTS ARE bigger and more powerful than children – yet children need constant care and make never-ending demands – it is easy for parenting to descend into ego-trips and power struggles: 'How can I stop my baby crying? How do I get my child off to sleep quickly? How do I get them to eat healthy foods? How do I stop them squabbling? How can I control my "hyperactive" child? How do I make my teenagers come home on time?' And so on.

As soon as you try to control your children, you're heading for problems. You are teaching them that relationships are based on power struggles – so naturally enough, they will fight back and strive to manipulate or dominate *you*! (Or they might express their rage by bullying other children, torturing animals, lying, stealing or joyriding – or by being depressed, or failing at school.) Parents who aim for domination are afraid of losing control, and have not learnt to see children as *people*. Instead they see parenting as a battleground in which they have to fight to win. Many of them were abused as children themselves, and their power struggle often leads to emotional or physical abuse of their own children. ('You will do it *because I tell you to!*' 'Don't talk back to me!' 'Get in your room and stay there!')

Of course, parents do need to set limits and boundaries for children: 'You can draw on paper, but not on walls', 'You can stay out until eight o'clock', 'You can have one packet of crisps'. There is nothing wrong with this; in fact, it helps children to feel safe and secure, rather like playing a game in which the rules are familiar. However the rules need to be *flexible* and *loving*. Children are not stupid. Even young children know when a rule is caring or sensible, and when it is a power struggle. (I know of a family where the 16-year-old daughter is forced to eat every meal with a knife and fork 'because it's good table manners'. Needless to say, she rebels over this pointless rule, and mealtimes are miserable for the whole family.)

Children are not our possessions. They are merely on loan to us while they grow up and become independent. *We have no right to punish or control our children* – any more than we have the right to punish or control our spouse or a neighbour.

If we support our children in making decisions, they develop a healthy sense of empowerment, and learn how to make choices that are right *for them*. (At the age of two, Kieran often chooses what to wear. Gone are the days of coordinated outfits; today he chose a red top, lime-green trousers and purple socks! But his power to choose is far more important than my concern over colour-matching. However, if he wants to go out in the snow without a coat, the answer is a gentle but firm No.)

Many children today are passive from dawn to dusk – having little choice over their school timetable, what to wear (school uniform), what to eat (meals are put on the table) or how to spend their free time ('Stay here so I can keep an eye on you'). Often their biggest decision of the day is which TV channel to watch – yet we expect them to grow up with the ability to be proactive and take charge of their own lives. (Research suggests that home-educated children, who play an active role in planning their days and deciding what and when to learn, grow up far more self-confident, independent and self-motivating.)

Even if it is uncomfortable at times, or doesn't fit with what we think is best for our child – perhaps *we* feel embarrassed by having a teenager with pink hair, but it is *her* hair – we must support them in making decisions and taking the consequences, so that they learn to go within and consult their deep Self.

I support my child(ren) in making choices.

4

Work

1 · FOLLOW YOUR BLISS

IF THERE IS one golden rule for shifting work into Soft Time, it is this: *Follow your bliss*. Our work is our 'livelihood'; it should make us feel lively, energised, vital, joyful. It should feed our heart and soul – allowing us to give and receive love, to express our creativity, to develop wisdom and compassion, to become more of who we are. If you don't leap out of bed on a Monday morning, eager to get on with your day, you're not yet doing your life's work.

For many people, work is a necessary evil, a means of paying the bills. It is merely a 'job'. Our ego-self goes to work because it is slightly preferable to living on benefits, because it fears the alternative, because it needs 'security'. It often feels pressurised, anxious and out of control at work – or just plain bored – and focuses on mere survival. More heart attacks occur between 8am and 9am on Monday morning than at any other time; returning to a 'heartless' job tears us apart.

Work is supposed to be about joy, delight, passion, love, vision, creativity, enthusiasm, play, sharing, inspiration. It is the sacred expression of our deep Self. It is meant to be pure bliss. (If you won the lottery, would you still do the work you are doing now? If not, you're not yet following your bliss.)

A true 'livelihood' frees us to express our inner Child. It feels like coming home to ourselves. Many people put on a professional 'mask' at work, hiding their real self until they get home – but being dour and serious means we have far less impact. If we are over-controlled and 'stuck in our head', if we do not speak from the heart, others sense our lack of honesty and integrity – and it turns them off. The playfulness, spontaneity and passion of our inner Child are essential at work.

What do you really love doing? What makes your heart expand, and fills you with delight? What feels like an enjoyable challenge? Do you love meeting new people? Or having intimate discussions? Or playing with colours, designs, textures? Or walking in the woods? Or being with your dog? Or juggling with abstract ideas? Or making music? Or reading about spiritual growth? Or putting up shelves? Or standing in front of an audience? Or ice-skating? Or telling stories to children? Or gardening? Or driving? Or gazing up at the stars? What do you love most about these activities? When you were a child, how did you spend your free time (apart from watching TV)? If you could do anything for a living, without having to worry about making an income, what would you do? (If you have no idea what you enjoy, try *anything* – try something new each week – until you discover what you love.)

It's also worth considering your ideal *lifestyle*. Do you enjoy living in the city or the country? Do you like routine, or prefer flexible working hours? Would you like to work as part of a team, or on your own? Do you thrive on pressure and deadlines, or prefer to work at your own pace? Do you adore travelling, or are you a home-bird? How much time do you want to devote to work? If you described your ideal lifestyle right now — and it will probably change over time — what would it be? Doing your life's work will allow you to develop that lifestyle.

By following our heart, we are gradually led towards our true work. It is often like piecing together a jigsaw puzzle of knowledge, experiences, personal qualities, strengths and vision — until it emerges like a butterfly from its chrysalis, and we see the whole picture. At first, it might be unclear how to make a living from it — but if we trust in the Universe, it will lead us wherever we need to go.

I do what I love.

2 · RELEASE NEGATIVE BELIEFS ABOUT WORK

MARIANNE QUICKLY CHANGED her job three times because she found her bosses critical and unsupportive. 'I tried so hard, and I just wanted to feel appreciated', she said. She felt optimistic as she started her fourth job in 18 months, because a friend shared the same boss and found him very affirming and supportive. To her dismay, Marianne was called to his office after a month, and told that she had some 'areas for improvement'! At first, she felt crushed – but she finally got the message. The world of work was simply mirroring back her own beliefs and expectations – and until she changed *herself*, every boss would be the same.

Many of us have the fantasy that if only we found the perfect job, the ideal office-space, wonderful colleagues or the longed-for promotion, we would be happy at work. The reality is that changing our job is far less important than changing our beliefs and attitudes. The outside world is a mirror – so we cannot move from a job we hate to a job we love unless we transform *ourselves* in the meantime.

If you feel bored or dissatisfied at work, here are some questions to consider:

- What do you see as the purpose of work? (e.g. to earn money, to feel good about yourself, to make a contribution to society, to express yourself).

- What beliefs and attitudes about work did you absorb in childhood? (e.g. 'Thank God it's Friday!', 'It's not much of a job, but at least it's secure', 'You never know when your job might be on the line', 'It's a tough job but someone has to do it', 'You have to sacrifice your home life to succeed'). Did the adults around you work hard for little reward? Did they enjoy their work, or endure it?

- How do your friends and colleagues see work? Do you surround yourself with people who hate work, feel indifferent – or love it?

- How did you choose your current job, trade or profession? (Suggestion from a parent or teacher? Just what was on offer? Or was it a heartfelt Dream?) What are your beliefs about this job – and how do you 'prove' these beliefs to yourself?

- Imagine you have your Dream job. You look forward to starting work each day, and feel a warm glow of satisfaction when you finish for the evening. How would this work differ from your current job? And what would you have to believe about yourself, or about work, in order to attract this Dream job?

Your beliefs are not sculpted in stone. You can change them – and far more easily than you might imagine! The first step is to become aware of your current beliefs – and to shift from *identifying* with those beliefs ('This is how the world is') to merely *witnessing* them ('This is what part of me believes'). Secondly, you have to recognise any possible payoffs for hanging on to those old beliefs – such as self-pity and martyrhood, gaining approval from others, proving your parents right (or wrong), or avoiding the risk of failure (or success); and you have to be willing to change your old beliefs, and give up these payoffs. Thirdly, you need to substitute positive new beliefs – and keep reminding yourself of these new beliefs until they feel 'obvious', and the outside world starts to mirror them back.

Here are a few positive affirmations about work:

- I deserve to be happy and fulfilled at work.
- My uniqueness is my gift to the world.
- The Universe totally supports me in doing what I love.
- Success comes to me easily and effortlessly.

My work is pure bliss!

3 · KNOW YOUR HIGHER PURPOSE

REAL WORK IS not just a way of earning a living, or filling our time. It is part of our soul's chosen destiny – and *it makes a difference*.

There are three major clues to our higher purpose:

- **Our work experience and background.** We might have several 'jobs', and perhaps train for one or more careers, *en route* to our life's work. I was a freelance writer for several years, then a clinical psychologist for a decade, while privately pursuing my spiritual path – before combining all of these in my thirties to become a spiritual writer and teacher. (The 'classic' age for discovering our life's work is 33, as in my case – but some people know their path early in life; or if you need a lot of different skills or qualities, it could be much later.)
- **Our strengths and talents, and what we love doing.** As the mystic poet Rumi said, 'Everyone has been called for some particular work, and the desire for that work has been put in their heart'.
- **Our global visions: how we most want to see the world change.** I believe that everyone has their own unique role to play in the planetary transformation that is

taking place, that we are each drawn to changing the world in a particular way. It can be exciting to recognise that our life's work is a small but essential piece in a giant jigsaw puzzle!

The global shift in consciousness – letting go of Hard Time – can be seen as a return of the Goddess, or a re-balancing of masculine/feminine energy on the planet. Your own higher purpose might fit into one or more of these 12 categories – each of which reflects the return of the divine feminine:

1. Healing the split between matter and spirit; bringing the sacred into everyday life; reclaiming the mystical side of religion.
2. Reclaiming our 'feminine' energy as individuals: e.g. helping people develop their intuition and psychic skills, or to move beyond co-dependency, martyrhood, fear and struggle, or to 'see the bigger picture'.
3. Breaking down the walls of separation and judgement: e.g. tackling racism, ageism, homophobia, nationalism, religious fundamentalism.
4. Working on women's issues: e.g. women's rights, redefining 'femininity'.
5. Working on behalf of children: e.g. preventing child abuse, supporting children's self-esteem and inner wisdom, campaigning for children's rights.
6. Honouring emotions and the inner Child: e.g. as a psychotherapist or teacher.
7. Honouring the physical body: e.g. health reform,

re-spiritualising sexuality.

8. Bringing Spirit back into business, town planning, architecture, the law, education and other social systems.

9. Reclaiming the holistic world view – that is, seeing wholes/systems rather than parts: e.g. as economist, ecologist, holistic health practitioner, family therapist.

10. Working with imagination and creativity: e.g. as an artist, playwright, storyteller, teacher, clown, designer.

11. Supporting co-operation rather than competition: e.g. divorce mediation; international diplomacy; working co-creatively with angels and guides.

12. Honouring the Earth and the natural world: e.g. ecological activism; shamanic wisdom; working with nature spirits; working with animals, plants or minerals in respectful ways; organising pilgrimages to sacred places.

I am willing to make a difference.

4 · STOP EFFORTING!

A FRIEND WHO works as a management consultant found that he was travelling long distances to see potential new clients, considering their issues in detail, sending them free reports – then being offered a day or two's consultancy in return. It was all too much effort for too little return! He knew he must be sabotaging himself, and eventually realised that – because of his family background – he believed that it was difficult to get well-paid work, and that we have to struggle hard to 'earn' it. He firmly decided to 'stop efforting' and allow work to come in easily – and soon after, he was offered an international contract which transformed his business.

'Stop efforting' is a golden rule for working in Soft Time. If it feels like an effort, you're working in Hard Time – so you will be less efficient, less creative, less productive, make more mistakes and enjoy it less. You will probably be stuck in martyrhood, and it will feel like walking uphill through thick treacle.

'Working hard' invariably means wasting a lot of time on unnecessary or pointless tasks, since you have lost perspective on what really matters, and what should be ignored, postponed or delegated. After a day of busywork, you feel empty and dissatisfied, and instead of relaxing to recharge your batteries, and tune into your higher wisdom, you might plough on regardless and become more and more exhausted – or perhaps resort to having a few drinks to 'unwind'.

When we're in Soft Time, by contrast, everything flows. It feels like being carried along by a gently-flowing river. We are highly creative and productive, focus on our true priorities, and produce our peak performance at any task. Work feels easy and effortless. It might require concentration, yes – but that's easy when you're in the flow, since you're totally present in the moment. It might be challenging, yes – but that's enjoyable in Soft Time, since we choose our own challenges, thrive on self-development and love what we do. As Nick Williams notes, 'work is only hard when it is without love'.[1]

One of the gifts of living in Soft Time is that we slip naturally into a slower rhythm, and begin to see overwork as a waste of time. We know that working long hours, day after day, does not pay – that work has to follow the rhythms of nature, that it is essential to have fallow periods to produce a good harvest, that a balanced lifestyle is reflected positively in our work, that we cannot hear our inner wisdom in the midst of frantic busyness.

Living in Soft Time means that work and play are no longer separate activities. We are often playful and child-like at work; and our most productive 'work periods' – when we come up with breakthrough ideas – might be while walking in a wood, or soaking in the bath, or flying a kite, or just before falling asleep at night. One friend is most creative when he's on the move – so if he has to come up with ideas, he goes for a walk. Another friend sits on a particular park bench near her office, which has become her personal 'power spot' for vision and inspiration. The idea for this book came to me while on holiday on the isle of Arran – and my husband and I often have our best ideas while taking 'time out' at our Cornish cottage.

One of the myths of Hard Time is that success only comes through hard work and gritted teeth. (If you arrive early for a meeting, or have time to linger afterwards, you're clearly not busy enough – says our Hard Time self!) The reality is that if we 'stop efforting' and follow our energy, we achieve far more – *and* we enjoy it.

I relax – and let my work flow.

5 · Beware of Work Addiction

THE ONLY PROBLEM with doing work we love is that our passion can become an addiction. In '*Working Ourselves to Death*', Diane Fassel notes that, 'Everywhere I go it seems people are killing themselves with work, busyness, rushing, caring, and rescuing. Work addiction is a modern epidemic ...'[2]. Work has become a substitute for living, a form of escapism. The problem is that, like compulsive caring, being a workaholic is a 'respectable' addiction which is socially sanctioned and often goes unrecognised.

Most workaholics, like other addicts, deny there is any problem. 'I just love my work – it really gives me a buzz.' 'I'm going to work hard for a few more years, then retire early.' 'My boss expects it.' 'Everyone works long hours in my job.' 'It's just while the business gets on its feet.' 'I'm working hard for my kids.'

Characteristically, workaholics have shaky self-esteem and a strong need to be in control, yet they need recognition or approval from others. They are perfectionists, unable to relax and rather obsessional. They fail to take care of their own needs, sometimes to the point of self-abuse, avoid intimacy and are often socially isolated. Often they have other addictions – such as shopping compulsively to 'compensate' for working so hard, drinking every night, over-eating or dieting, smoking or compulsive exercising.

The underlying problem is that workaholics have become estranged from their deep Self, and are looking to the outside world to meet needs which can only be met from within – and I know from my own experience that we can slip into exhausting busyness even when we meditate daily and are highly committed to personal and spiritual growth. (In my own case, I eventually realised that I valued my work more than I valued myself – and it was time to redress the balance. I also had a long-standing belief that successful people are busy, so I gave myself a new affirmation: *Success means a balanced lifestyle.*)

Giveaway signs that you are becoming workaholic might be that work comes to fill all the available spaces in your life – so that you are 'living to work', rather than 'working to live'; that intimacy becomes a dim and distant memory; that you forget what you really enjoy because it's so long since you did it; that your life feels chronically out of balance; that you can't remember how old your children are; or that you find yourself denying to others that you are a workaholic!

When you start to give up work addiction, suppressed emotions, insights and desires often come to the surface – and you might have to get to know yourself all over again. Often you have to face 'the void' – feelings of emptiness or nothingness, low self-esteem, not knowing what direction to take, feeling hopeless or even despairing. It might even mean being unemployed for a while, or at most working part-time, so that you can rediscover who 'you' are apart from your work. You might need to resist the urge to fill your days with 'busyness' — redecorating the house, land-scaping the garden, applying for hundreds of jobs, becoming a full-time volunteer — and allow yourself time simply to be. It is a period when silence, solitude and stillness are essential, so that you get in touch with your deep Self again. It can be a scary and exhilarating time.

Success means a balanced lifestyle.

6 · Focus on What Really Matters

If you spent just *one or two hours* each day focusing on your top work priority – which might be writing a novel, drafting designs, brainstorming ideas, studying Spanish or converting your loft into an office – you would be amazed at your progress! Weeks or months can easily slip past without acting on our priorities if we wait 'until we have more time' – and in the meantime, we give the message to the Universe that our priorities lie elsewhere.

Time management experts reckon that the majority of our work-time is devoted to tasks which are 'urgent but not important' – such as reading mail, answering phone calls, filling in forms or dealing with petty crises. Instead we should focus more on what is 'important but not urgent': planning, preparation, visioning, relationship-building, our true work.

I find that I'm far more productive now that I have a toddler to care for, since I have only 2–4 hours free each day – so I am far more focused during work-time. My top priority is writing, so I always *start* my work periods by writing. Only when I'm ready for a break do I turn to routine tasks such as paying bills or ordering stationery. (When I handled routine jobs first 'to get them out of the way', I found they took up most of the available time.)

When we're in Hard Time, we get easily sidetracked by lists of tasks, messages and details, and fail to see that all the 'little jobs' can usually wait – perhaps forever. Many of us confuse busyness with being valued, important or virtuous – or we imagine that being busy means being productive – so we frantically dash about doing this and that, hoping for a sense of achievement and satisfaction when we finally find time to stop and catch our breath. In fact, we rarely feel fulfilled since we're not focusing on what really matters; instead we feel exhausted and empty.

In Soft Time, our vision is more expansive, and we are guided by our passion. We clarify our vision – what we intend to do, what we hope to offer, how we hope to help change the world – then we build our working time around that vision. In Soft Time, we 'work smarter, not harder'.

Our true work is often guided by our inner work. We teach what we need to learn, so we often give others advice that we need to give ourselves! We discover ourselves through our work – and as we grow and change, so does our outer work. Our livelihood becomes a thrilling voyage of self-discovery and self-expression – and through our own journey, we help others to evolve. As Matthew Fox puts it, 'Our work takes on a cosmic significance when it is inner work'.

If you need to clarify what really matters in your work, try asking yourself:

• What do I do that makes a difference? (It might not be the specific goods or services you offer, but the fact that you radiate love and joy in providing them.)

- What am I learning about myself through my outer work?
- What do I see as my true work, my livelihood, my passion?
- What feels most exciting and challenging in my work?
- What can I offer that uniquely expresses who I am?
- What is my long-term vision for my work? Where am I going?
- And what are my current short-term plans for moving towards that vision?
- If I had only one or two hours to work each day, what would I focus upon?

I focus on what really matters.

7 · DEAL WITH ONE TASK AT A TIME

MOST OF THE pressure in work situations comes not from deadlines, or others' expectations, or having too much to do – but from inside our own head. Let's suppose you have 50 letters to reply to this morning. The chances are that you keep looking over at the pile, wondering how you'll get through it all, glancing at the next letters while replying to this one, hurrying as fast as you can, feeling overwhelmed – and kicking yourself for taking on this job in the first place. When your head is full of busyness, you cannot think or act clearly, since your fearful and negative thoughts distract you from the task in hand. A stressed worker is an inefficient worker.

Alternatively you might reach for one letter at a time, calmly read and reply to it – then reach for the next letter. This way, all you have to do is answer *this* letter. Then *this* one. Then *this* one. You're no longer trying to be super-human, and deal with 50 letters all at once! You are calm, focused and efficient, since you're living in Soft Time. If we focus on what we are doing *right now* – rather than on the countless tasks which lie ahead – our stress levels are dramatically reduced, and the quality of our work is far higher.

When we're living in the Soft Time cycle, it always *feels* as if there is plenty of time – since we are fully present in the moment, and free from the stress of frantic busyness. Our perception of time changes in the most miraculous way.

A useful tip which I learnt from Richard Carlson[3] is to be aware of your own 'stacking order'. Our stacking order is the number of ongoing projects which we feel happiest with at any one time – and it can help us stay in Soft Time. Some people like to throw themselves into a single project, and carry on until it is done. Others find they go crazy unless they have several projects on the go, so that they can switch to something different if they want a change. I like to have three or four work projects at a time. (I get bored with a single project, and feel scattered if I have more than four.) At the moment, I'm working on this book, self-help tapes for children, and my next brochure. If something new comes up which needs my attention for a while, I put a project in my stacking order 'on hold' until the new one is completed. At the start of each week, I decide roughly how much time I want to devote to each project, and what I aim to do that week. (If you're a book-lover, think about how many books you like to have 'on the go'; that might give you a clue about the number in your stacking order.)

Another invaluable tip that I use is to keep your desk clear.[4] If your desk is cluttered with papers and folders, reminders about this and that, phone messages and unanswered letters, your head will feel equally cluttered – and it will be difficult to work effectively. Instead keep all of your plans, ideas, notes and reminders in one notebook – and file or throw away *everything* else. Studies of highly successful people show that they usually have a clear desk — empty apart from the letter, issue or file they are dealing with *right now*. Less successful people have cluttered desks which demonstrate how 'busy' they are — and how stuck they are in Hard Time!

*I am fully present in **this** moment.*

8 · BREAK THE RULES!

WHEN I COMPLETED my first book, *Living Magically*, the accepted practice was to send a manuscript to one publisher at a time, allowing at least three months for a decision – so it sometimes took years to find a publisher. Author Guy Dauncey phoned me at that time, and said: 'Don't be afraid to break the rules! Send it to several publishers at once.' I shall always be grateful for that advice. It was just what I longed to do! I sent my manuscript to five publishers, telling each of them I was doing so – and three months later, the *fifth* publisher on my shortlist (Piatkus) offered me a contract.

Breaking the rules is a way of liberating ourselves from social norms which are unhelpful and limiting. It does not mean 'acting out' in a rebellious, adolescent way, or being nonconformist for the hell of it. It means being free to follow your heart, and discover your own way of doing things. It might mean questioning accepted practices, disregarding the conventions of how to succeed in your chosen career, and refusing to copy anyone else's version of 'success'.

Seth reminds us that 'No apple tree tries to grow violets'[5] – yet many people strive to be more like others, to fit in with what is expected, to be different from who they are. The paradox is that when we try to conform or copy others, we become a pale imitation of who we might be. (I once knew a skilled artist who made copies of well-known paintings. Although he made a good living, he felt he was wasting his talent since he wasn't discovering *himself* as an artist.) What really makes us sparkle and shine is our uniqueness. We can learn from others, certainly – even use them as role models in the early stages of our life's work. But fulfilling our potential means expressing our individuality: being bold, being brave, being different.

Aviva Gold[6] tells the story of an art teacher who attended a 'painting from the source' workshop. At the age of 50, Betty was wrestling with the issue of ageing: whether to try to conceal her grey hair and wrinkles (as society urged her to) or to embrace and celebrate her ageing (as she wished to). She began by painting a shapely female silhouette and other pretty figures in swirling bright colours. She produced a beautiful painting which she could easily have sold – but she felt uncomfortable with it, as if she was 'selling out', following the rules. After a long struggle, she dipped her brush in black paint and – amidst gasps from the rest of the workshop – covered the entire painting in black. Then she carried on painting. What finally emerged was a stunning, vibrant image of a shaman's wide open mouth, through which white skeletons came dancing out. It was a bold, riveting vision – a true expression of her wild Self, her deep Self.

When we are willing to break the rules, to forge our own path, to take 'the road less travelled by', we no longer feel driven to compete, or to compare ourselves with others.

Instead our sense of self-worth comes from *inside* – from listening to our heart, from being true to ourselves. We co-operate wholeheartedly with others, but 'compete' only with ourselves – aiming for excellence, aiming for elegance, aiming for self-expression.

I am willing to be bold. I follow my own path.

9 · Remember the Power of Silence

Silence can be a powerful ally in the workplace. Amidst the hustle and bustle of a busy office, it offers a way of shifting into Soft Time and connecting with our inner wisdom and power.

If you allow yourself five or ten minutes of silence at the start of a working day – either reflecting calmly on your plans for the day ahead, or asking your deep Self 'What do I need to know right now?', or simply allowing your mind to be still – you will be amazed at how much time and effort it saves in the long term. New ideas might bubble up, or a fresh perspective on a work issue, or a reminder about something that needs to be done, or inner guidance about a work project. Or you might simply feel calmer and more relaxed, so that you bypass the small-minded and muddy thinking that accompanies pressure, rushing and busyness – and so 'work smarter' all day.

For some years, I was a regular attender at Quaker meetings, in which silence is the norm and people speak only when they feel moved to do so – often sharing a personal experience or a reading along with their reflections on its deeper significance. The words that emerged from that profound silence and stillness were so often wise and memorable – and sometimes addressed my private musings with astonishing synchronicity. The Quakers are natural mystics who have always been aware of the power of silence, and the Light within us.

Whenever you find yourself under stress at work – and especially when you feel you 'haven't time' to take a few minutes out – give yourself the gift of silence. Lock yourself in the bathroom if necessary! Emerge only when you've shifted into a calmer state of mind – *then* return to the task in hand. You will have a different approach and a clear head, and will probably wonder what you were getting so steamed up about!

Another option is to use the NLP (neuro-linguistic programming) technique of 'anchoring'. Relax deeply and sink into the silence. Once you feel deliciously calm and peaceful, make a simple physical gesture such as pulling your left earlobe, or touching your right thumb against your middle finger. (Choose a gesture which you can use unobtrusively in the presence of others.) Next time you feel caught up in busyness, or under pressure from deadlines, repeat the gesture in exactly the same way in order to feel calm and relaxed again.

Silence can also work miracles in a committee or business meeting – especially where there is a conflict of views. Some colleagues might view it as a 'waste of time' to begin with a short period of silence – but they will change their minds if they experience what happens! I once attended a committee meeting for a voluntary group where disagreements over how to spend a large donation were becoming almost aggressive. We agreed to have five minutes of silence while we all 'calmed down'. Afterwards the discussion was quickly resolved amidst a lot of laughter.

Silence can dissipate the chitter-chatter of the ego-self, and allow us to move beyond petty concerns, fault-finding and negativity. In the stillness, our deep Self can step forward – with its open-hearted acceptance, its wisdom and humour, its creativity, vision and intuitive knowing. It is pure magic!

I listen to the still small voice within.

10 · FENG SHUI YOUR OFFICE

FENG SHUI IS the ancient Chinese art of placement, which helps create a balanced and harmonious environment, with a positive flow of energy (*Ch'i*). In the workplace, feng shui can help to increase your energy, aid concentration, boost your creativity, improve working relationships and attract prosperity. It might seem crazy to suggest that a mirror or fish tank, strategically placed, can dramatically affect your business or career – but people and corporations use it worldwide because it works! Everything is connected – and since inner and outer mirror each other, harmony in your environment does have an impact on your mind, body and spirit. Feng shui is a way of changing your life from the 'outside in', and designing your surroundings to support your Dreams and visions.

If you avoid spending time in your office, often feel tired, depressed or confused there, if office relations are strained or work isn't going as well as you feel it should – or you just wish to maximise your potential at work – try feng shui.

Here are a few tips to get you started:

- Move anything that obstructs the doorway to your office, so that it feels easy and comfortable to walk in.

- Arrange your workspace so that it 'feels' balanced and harmonious.
- Your desk position is crucial. Make sure you can see the door while seated at your desk, without facing it directly. Ideally sit with your back to a wall, diagonally opposite the door. Avoid having a window behind you, or you'll feel unsupported; or having shelves above your desk, as you'll feel pressurised; or being near the door, or you might leave your job sooner than expected!
- Soften an overstimulating, busy or bright-coloured office by adding plants, personal photos, cushions, pictures of nature.
- Get rid of clutter. It drains your energy, scatters your thinking and prevents you from moving on. Throw away piles of paper, files and other clutter – and file anything you really do need. Don't use feng shui 'enhancements' (such as windchimes) in a cluttered space, or you'll just increase the problems.
- To enhance the energy, add: clear light, healthy plants, fresh flowers, water (such as a *clean* fish tank, fountain, picture of lake or ocean), pets, hanging crystals or mirrors. Cleaning, vacuuming and redecorating also clear energy.
- Avoid: harsh light (e.g. fluorescent light, too much direct sun), lack of light, sharp corners facing you, long narrow corridors, dead or dying plants.
- If you work at home, avoid using your bedroom as an office. The energies of working and sleeping are incompatible.
- Avoid open shelves, which give off sharp 'attacking' energy.

- Empty wastepaper bins every day.
- Balance lots of metal (filing cabinets and so on) with wood and plants.
- Create an indoor fountain using a large bowl, stones and a small water pump (from a garden centre). I have one in my office; it is a lovely sound – soothing yet invigorating – and water is a symbol of wealth.
- Use a plant spray to increase healthy negative ions in the air – perhaps adding a few drops of essential oil such as lemon or rosemary to lift your mood, or rose, jasmine or neroli for calmness. (Computers, faxes, photocopiers and so on emit positive ions and many other kinds of radiation.) Healthy vigorous plants clear the air too; peace lilies are particularly good.
- Hang a crystal over your phone if you want to attract phone-calls.
- Choose paintings or pictures for your office which are positive, inspiring and give you a lift whenever you look at them. Throw out any others!
- According to feng shui, every room or house can be divided into eight areas which correspond to different aspects of our lives. Consider your office (or desk), and enhance the areas of the *bagua* which correspond to career, fame, wealth, creativity or helpful people – or whichever feels most important to you. Clear clutter, then energise the area with the items or colours given below.

Prosperity	Fame	Love & Marriage
Family & Health		Creativity & Children
Knowledge & Personal Growth	Career	Helpful People & Travel

↑   ↑

Entrance door (or front of desk) along this side.

The Bagua

CAREER (front middle) – Water features, pictures of water; mirrors, glass, crystal; images of your career or success; affirmations about your career; black, navy and dark-coloured objects; random or freeform shapes.

FAME (rear middle) – Awards, diplomas etc.; photos of famous people you admire; pictures of fire/volcano/sun; candles; lights; birds; pyramid/triangle shapes; number 9; colour red.

PROSPERITY (rear left) – Any valuable or gold objects; old coins; windchimes; plants with coin-shaped leaves; fish; pictures of what you want; affirmations about money;

number 4; colours purple, blue and red.

CREATIVITY (middle right) – Photos of children; art by children; stuffed toys and childhood memorabilia; art supplies; circular, oval or arched objects; round or curvy desk; metal; number 7; white and pastel colours.

HELPFUL PEOPLE & TRAVEL (front right) – Pictures of angels, saints, gods or goddesses, or helpful people in your life; spiritual items; helpful quotations; photos of places you love, or wish to visit; colours white, grey and black.

PARTNER (rear right) – To attract a business partner or improve a partnership, add matched pairs of objects or something yellow in the Marriage area of your desk or office.

My outer world mirrors my inner world.

5

Money

1 · DEVELOP YOUR INNER PROSPERITY

MY FAVOURITE DEFINITION of prosperity is 'living easily and happily in the world'. It reminds us that prosperity is not about having a fat bank account, or a home dripping with antiques and valuable paintings. Many of the wealthiest people in the world are not prosperous at all. Billionaire Howard Hughes dying of malnutrition provided a striking image of a 'poor rich man', and I have met many wealthy people who are anxious and driven about money. On the other hand, I spent a day with an ever-smiling Buddhist monk in Thailand who owned nothing – and was truly prosperous. Our inner prosperity bears little relation to our actual wealth.

We often assume that having money and possessions will make us feel prosperous and secure, but true prosperity does not come from outside the self. It comes from our deep Self, from living in Soft Time. Prosperity is a state of mind, not a bank balance. It means feeling safe, secure and relaxed in the world, and having a sense of freedom and abundance. It means never worrying about money, since we trust that the Universe will provide whatever we need – and since the world mirrors back our inner prosperity, it means we also attract money and other resources more easily.

In order to develop inner prosperity, imagine that you are financially prosperous and picture your lifestyle. Where do you live? What do you surround yourself with? How do you spend your time? Imagine it vividly, using all your senses. Then focus on how you *feel*. How does it feel to be prosperous? That *feeling* of prosperity is what you need to cultivate – and you can have the *feeling* right away!

The next step is to act 'as if' you are prosperous. This does *not* mean splashing out and taking your credit cards to their limit! When we falsely associate prosperity with money, we often spend compulsively in the belief that it will make us feel more prosperous; this creates a vicious circle in which the 'solution' becomes part of the problem. Remember that prosperity has little to do with money!

Acting 'as if' means changing your lifestyle – often in small ways – to give yourself that crucial inner *feeling* of prosperity. If you were living easily and happily in the world, how would your life be different? Perhaps you would make time for leisure activities which you tell yourself you're 'too busy' to enjoy. (My prosperous self goes for long walks in the country, plays the guitar, reads poetry and has an occasional snooze in the afternoon.) Perhaps you would throw out junk furniture or cheap-and-cheerful clothes, and buy a few quality items you can afford. Perhaps you would relax more with friends and loved ones, or travel more, or keep fresh flowers in your home. Whatever it means, do it *now!*

Prosperity is not *all* in the mind; unless you live in a monastery, money certainly comes in handy! But unless you have *inner* prosperity, you will be unable to make the most of money and other resources. You will not attract money easily, and will anxiously cling to your savings 'just in case' – instead of using them to enrich your life. I know a woman who has saved every penny she can during her 40-year marriage 'just in case' her husband leaves her one day. Amazingly, he hasn't – but money has always been a focus for her chronic insecurity.

Many of us fantasise about winning the lottery or inheriting a fortune from a long-lost aunt – but the truth is that what we are hoping for is not the money, but the *feeling* of relaxation, security, freedom, joy, power, expansion of possibilities, growth. We are yearning for something that is available right now – inside us!

I live easily and happily in the world.

2 · Take the 'Weight' out of Money

Money is a powerful symbol in our society. It provides us with the basic necessities – food, shelter, clothing – so it is a symbol of security and having our needs met. Others give it in exchange for our time, skills or services – so it is also a symbol of self-worth and self-esteem. It can buy us leisure time and experiences – so it is a symbol of freedom and choice. It can be swapped for 'status symbols' and badges of identity – so it is also a symbol of personal identity and belonging. And it can be heavily linked with our relationships with our parents, partner or ex-partners – becoming a symbol of love, support, dependence, neediness and power. No wonder we can get so screwed up about money – it means so much to us!

Our approach to money often reveals how safe and secure we feel in the world, or how emotionally needy we are. If we worry about money, or have a compulsive desire to spend, or obsessively 'safeguard' our future, or daydream about being rich, or feel guilty about having or spending money, it shows that money symbolises other issues in our lives.

Many years ago, I worked with women with eating disorders – and I was struck by the similarities between food and money. Like money, food and body weight are heavily 'weighted' in our society, so that eating a cream cake is no longer just eating a cream cake: it might 'mean' losing control, or rewarding yourself, or being wicked, or nourishing your inner Child, or protecting yourself, or punishing someone. Similarly, some people have anorexic or bulimic spending habits – either chronically depriving themselves or compulsively binge-spending. Money *and* food are often seen as 'bad but desirable', and expected to meet emotional needs which they can never fulfil – which means you *never* feel rich enough (or thin enough).

One key to prosperity is to release the 'weight' you have attached to money. Imagine that you have as much money as you could ever want or need – and notice how it feels. Then ask:

- What does money seem to symbolise to you? Security, freedom, independence, power, status, self-worth, happiness, having your emotional needs met?
- Does it feel scary to be rich? If so, what do you fear others might expect from you if you were rich? What might you expect yourself to do? Do you currently use lack of money as an excuse? What do you tell yourself you would do 'if only you could afford it'? Is money the *real* reason? Be honest!
- Do you associate money with your parents, or an ex-partner? Imagine telling them you are wealthy. Do you feel any anxiety or resistance? Would you be 'letting them down' in some way by being rich? Or letting them off the hook?
- If you have a partner, do you ever squabble over money?

If so, what does money symbolise within this relation-ship? Power? Neediness? Trust? Dependence?

Once you know what money symbolises to you, and what fears you have about being wealthy, you can begin to release that 'weight'. You can commit yourself to finding security, or freedom, or self-worth, or power *within* yourself – rather than expecting money to meet those needs. If money is a symbol of freedom, what does it mean to you to be free? How might you begin to liberate yourself? Know that freedom is a gift we give ourselves; it is not something that money can provide.

Money is not a magic wand. It is just energy. It is paper, coins or electronic numbers. It is a useful resource. It can be exchanged for goods and experiences – but it cannot make us feel safe, happy or good about ourselves.

I feel secure (or free, or powerful . . .) however much money I have.

3 · HEAL YOUR ATTITUDE TOWARDS MONEY

IF YOU WANT to be prosperous, it's essential to have a positive attitude towards money. Do you feel a bit sheepish about admitting you want more money in your life? Do you associate wealth with greed, selfishness or materialism – or believe it is more spiritual to be poor? Do you undercharge for your goods or services? Or believe you shouldn't be paid for work you enjoy? Do you limit yourself to badly-paid jobs? Or give to charity from a sense of guilt? Do you believe that if you have more, others have less? If so, you have some healing work to do around money!

Yes, of course, money *can* be used to build bombs, cages or deadly chemicals – but the fact that it *can* be abused is not money's fault. It can also provide safe drinking water, build homes or save the rainforests – or can simply help us to have fun and enjoy life. Money is just energy – completely neutral in itself.

If you're puritanical or ambivalent about money, parts of you will magnetise it while other parts push it away. You might attract a small windfall, then find that your car needs mending – and the windfall just covers the repair bill. You will only apply for jobs with a salary within your 'comfort zone', or money will always go out as soon as it comes in, so that you never have a sense of abundance.

If you see money and spirituality as incompatible – and plenty of people do – you might believe that healing or spiritual work should be unpaid, since it is a 'gift from God'. This assumes that other work – such as shopkeeping, carpentry or dentistry – is *not* a gift from God! (Only our ego-self could make such a judgement.) Similarly, if we see work as 'service' to others, it can lead us into martyrhood or workaholism – since 'service' can mean self-sacrifice and self-denial, or trying to prove our self-worth by giving to others. It leaves us with a false choice over whether to choose 'worthy' work or well-paid work, and can lead to guilt over earning money. As I see it, no work is 'special'. *All* work is a gift from God/dess – and money is a way of staying in balance, giving in exchange for someone's time, experience and skills. It is an agreed way of saying 'Thank you – I appreciate what you offer.'

There is nothing unspiritual about money – and nothing spiritual about poverty. Being poor means that we have to focus on survival needs, and have no spare time or energy for personal or spiritual growth. Lack of money limits our lives, puts pressure on our family and friends, and means that many doors of opportunity are closed to us. If you are a nun or monk, you can be prosperous without money, since all your needs are provided for – but for most of us, money is an essential tool for leading a happy and fulfilled life.[1] (Of course, a life which is *focused* on making money has missed the point entirely! Money is a resource, not a goal in itself.)

Prosperity is our natural birthright, and I believe that we're not finished on the Earth plane until we have learnt how to create prosperity and abundance in our lives. This does not mean we have to be rich! It *does* mean having enough money to follow our Dreams – whether that means buying books or a computer, travelling across China, designing a garden, hang-gliding or living in a character cottage. It means having a sense of unlimited freedom, and access to whatever resources we need to fulfil our soul's destiny, and create our own heaven on earth.

Money is my friend.

4 · DON'T DO IT 'JUST FOR THE MONEY'

THE GOLDEN RULE for creating prosperity is to do what you love. (*See Chapter 4 on Work.*) If you agree to do anything 'just for the money', you're acting from your limited ego-self – which believes that money is in short supply, or that you have to suffer to make a living, or don't deserve to be prosperous, or that life is a struggle. Since you are acting from fear and negativity, you attract more of the same, so you then find it more difficult to earn money by doing what you love.

I knew this rule at a head level for many years – then I discovered from experience how true it is. After I left the Health Service and while my first book was in press, I earned next to nothing for a year or two. I was offered various opportunities to write articles for women's magazines, or lecture in clinical psychology to postgraduates – but I now saw myself as a 'metaphysical teacher/writer', and promised myself that I would say No to any other means of earning money. Occasionally I had to swallow hard as I refused a generous offer – but I trusted in the Universe to support me in doing my life's work. Of course, it always did so.

Three years later, I was earning half my income through

personal consultations, but realised that I no longer enjoyed these sessions as much as I had. After 15 years as a psychotherapist, I wanted to devote more time to writing and workshops, which were (and are) my real passion – so with some trepidation, I stopped seeing clients altogether. In the months that followed, my income from other sources soared, and I was soon earning twice as much as before. The Universe offers limitless abundance – and when we follow our heart, we attract money more easily.

On the other hand, people *can* sabotage themselves by taking 'leaps of faith' which come from the ego-self. I remember a striking young woman at one of my workshops who had resigned from her dull office job to become an artist – but she felt frustrated by her lack of progress. It turned out that she hadn't trained as an artist, nor had she devoted years to practising her skills. In fact, she was a complete beginner! 'But I was following my Dream!' she told me rather indignantly, when I suggested she might have acted prematurely in resigning from her day job. It turned out she lived at home, and was rebelling against her parents' pressure to become a secretary and hang on to a 'secure job' even if she hated it. We discussed moving towards her Dream in a step-by-step way – and she later wrote to say she'd found a secretarial post in an art college which she was truly enjoying, while she attended art classes in her free time.

Whatever you do to earn money, promise yourself not to do it with a heavy heart – otherwise you link earning money with struggle and martyrhood. Don't tell yourself that 'someone has to do it'! My belief is that when enough people refuse to do dreary, repetitive, stressful, ecologically unsound or antisocial jobs, such jobs will cease to exist – so you will be doing the planet a favour by saying No.

Many people become self-employed when they release their martyrhood around work, so that they can choose exactly when and what they do. Others redefine the job they already have, perhaps by changing their attitude, so that it becomes more creative and meaningful; or choose to work part-time. And others look for a post in which they can truly express their deep Self, and fulfil their higher purpose.

The Universe supports me in doing what I love.

5 · LET MONEY FLOW LIKE A SACRED RIVER

FOR YEARS AND years, I was hopelessly neurotic about money. I wore threadbare clothes, bought second-hand furniture and refused to buy a cup of tea in a café because it was cheaper to drink at home. I felt self-righteous about the fact that I never 'wasted' money, somehow imagining that I was doing the world a favour by depriving myself! Eventually I realised that I was limiting myself in *every* aspect of my life, and that I had to sort out my attitudes towards money . . . . It took me quite some time, but I gradually did so – and I can honestly say I haven't worried about money for many years. I have some quality clothes that I really love, visit teashops regularly – and always seem to have more than enough money. I'm far from wealthy, but I feel free to do whatever I choose, and my life feels truly prosperous.

Money can be seen as a river which flows all around the world. Some people cling to the riverbank, desperately thirsty yet fearful of getting their feet wet. Others paddle in shallow pools at the river's edge. Some cling to a single jug of water from the river, carefully rationing themselves; while others dive into the clear deep water, drinking their fill, offering water to others – and trusting in the flow of the river to carry them wherever they need to go.

In deep reality, there is limitless prosperity – endless love, endless time, endless money, endless energy. Shortages are only conjured up by our shared Hard Time awareness, which mirrors our belief in separateness and limitation. (When enough people are living in Soft Time, I believe we will discover ways of providing unlimited energy and resources which do not pollute and damage the Earth.)

Stepping into the river of abundance means having an open and relaxed attitude towards money, allowing it to flow freely in and out of our lives, always trusting there is more to come. However, it also means seeing money as a precious and sacred resource – to be used wisely, sacramentally, not frittered away carelessly.

Being abundant does not mean going into debt, with the woolly-minded attitude that 'the Universe will provide'; nor does it mean spending money as soon as it comes in. (On the contrary, savings are an affirmation that you have more money than you need – so they attract more money.) In Hard Time, we often get trapped in an addictive cycle of earn-and-spend, and our spending is driven and compulsive, or focused on unnecessary trivia. It stems not from feeling prosperous, but from 'poverty consciousness': the belief that there is not enough to go round, so you'd better spend while you can! It can also be an attempt to comfort your inner Child, or a response to the false Dreams of advertising: 'Buy this and change your life!'

If we view spending as a *sacred* activity, we take care over what we buy – ensuring that our spending is heart-centred, joyful and expansive. We love and appreciate what we own or buy; and when a bill arrives, we pay it immediately, feeling gratitude for the services or goods provided. (If we sigh or curse at those little brown envelopes which arrive in the post, or delay making payment, we affirm our lack of prosperity – and so push money away.)

Whenever we spend money – or give in other ways – we are contributing to someone else's prosperity. If we stand by on the riverbank, it just means that we have less to give to the world. It might be helpful to see yourself as a role model for living in Soft Time: beyond separateness, beyond limitation. Try stretching your prosperity limits, expanding your vision, dreaming the impossible Dream. How rich, how free, how wonderful will you allow your life to be?

I believe in limitless prosperity.

6

Health

1 · EXPECT TO BE HEALTHY

ACCORDING TO MYSTICAL wisdom, *we create our own bodies*. The so-called 'solid stuff' of our reality (which modern physics agrees is an illusion) is just energy, which dances to the tune of consciousness. Everything (including our body) is a by-product of consciousness. This turns our 'common-sense' assumptions about the world upside-down! It means that *our health and well-being reflect what is happening in our mind*. As Deepak Chopra puts it, 'Our cells are constantly eavesdropping on our thoughts and being changed by them'.[1] Thus, if we love life, appreciate our body and *expect* to be healthy, we send positive messages to every cell – and our organs, biochemistry and immune system function more effectively.

Carl Simonton, well-known for his holistic approach to cancer, found that expectation of full recovery was a much better predictor of eventual outcome than the severity of cancer. In other words, those who kept telling themselves that they would get better – and *believed* it – were far more likely to do so.[2] What is more, since all consciousness is connected, if we expect our loved ones to be healthy – or to recover from illness – it has a real impact. (For a fascinating look at the power of prayer in medicine, see Larry Dossey's *Healing Words*, HarperCollins, 1993.)

From the perspective of deep reality, it is the whole person, rather than the body, which 'holds' health or disease. Studies show that 'multiple personalities' might have insulin-dependent diabetes as one personality, while another personality *in the same body* has no trace of diabetes; or one personality might have epilepsy or allergies while another is unaffected; even scars or warts can appear or disappear as the person shifts into another personality![3] This shows that the body is not a fixed, objective reality; it is moulded by our changing thoughts, emotions and personality.

According to the biomedical model, illness is merely a dysfunction of the body, with no inherent meaning or purpose – and is best treated by 'experts' using drugs, radiation or surgery. Since mind and body are seen as separate, the *person* is almost invisible in modern medicine – a mere unfortunate appendage to a disease. The biomedical model is not 'wrong'; it is just a very limited perspective. It has allowed drugs and medical technology to develop rapidly – but at the expense of understanding what illness or disease *mean* for a person, and how health is created.

In 1992, Brandon Bays[4] was diagnosed with a football-sized pelvic tumour, and advised to have immediate surgery – yet she was determined to get well without medical intervention. Only six-and-a-half weeks later, she was pronounced to be in tip-top health, with no trace of any tumour. No surgery, no drugs, no radiation. If we are willing to take responsibility for our own health, and face up to whatever is necessary, we can heal ourselves of almost anything.

Every year, 98 per cent of the atoms in our body are replaced. Even our skeleton is renewed every three months

– so in order to remain ill, we have to instruct the healthy new cells to be sick! Instead we could consciously create health. It sounds amazing but – as Deepak Chopra says – at the level of quantum reality, '*anything in your body* can be changed with the flick of an intention'.[5]

I am radiant with health and well-being.

2 · PAY ATTENTION TO YOUR 'BODY LANGUAGE'

OUR BODY IS always our friend. Every symptom or illness – from a common cold to a heart attack – is a message or opportunity of some kind. More often than not, symptoms relate to an unresolved conflict or imbalance in your life, such as suppressed anger or grief, blaming others, refusing to change, living in the past or future, avoiding intimacy or pursuing a certain goal without honouring other needs.

The body is a wonderful mirror of what is happening in our lives, or what needs to happen. Chronic health problems often highlight major life issues which need to be tackled, while minor symptoms can draw our attention to emotions or conflicts which we've been ignoring. Almost always, there are many gentle 'whispers' (or warning signs) before the loud 'shout' of a major illness or serious accident.

The first step in dealing with any illness is to take responsibility for it, without taking the blame. If you *blame* yourself for your disease, you will make yourself even more ill! Taking responsibility means taking back your power. It means recognising that if you created an illness, you can *uncreate* it! In any case, an illness or accident doesn't necessarily mean you have done anything 'wrong'. It might simply be the most elegant way of learning certain lessons or making changes in your life. (A friend of mine decided to train for a new career while lying in a hospital bed. A man from one of my workshops met his wife, who was a nurse, through having a car accident.) If you see illness as a nuisance or a tragedy, *or* use it as an excuse to beat yourself up, then you have completely missed the point!

Although it is a mistake to over-simplify illness, there does seem to be a widely-shared 'body language' (and if a disease becomes epidemic, it symbolises a conflict or imbalance within the whole culture). Here are a few common patterns I've observed over the years:

Arthritis – Feeling stuck in a situation which needs to change, perhaps believing there is no alternative, or that other options might be even worse. Suppressed desire for freedom. Inflexible and rigid.

Asthma – Feeling stifled or smothered by a situation, and wanting it to go away.

Auto-immune diseases (e.g. cancer, arthritis, chronic fatigue) – Needing the approval of others. Refusing to feel your emotions.

Bone cancer – Feeling 'weary to the bone', or that the 'foundations' of your life have been shattered.

Bowel cancer – Not releasing negative emotions; 'keeping the past alive'.

Breast cancer – Lack of self-love and self-care. Nurturing others at own expense. Anger at someone who didn't love you enough.

Headache – Inner conflict over what you *want* to do versus what you believe you 'should' do.

Heart disease – Blockages around giving/receiving love. Not 'following your heart'. 'Losing heart' in life.

Low back pain – Feeling burdened with too much responsibility. Martyrhood.

Nausea/vomiting – Something you can't 'stomach'. Wanting to change a past event.

Neck pain – Who/what is a 'pain in the neck'? Fear of 'sticking your neck out'.

Skin disorders – Often connected with poor self-image, how we 'face' the world. Weeping skin – suppressed grief; red, inflamed skin – suppressed anger.

If you're unsure what your illness means, one technique is to write to yourself as if you were the symptom, *using the hand you do not normally write with*, so that you bypass your rational mind. You might be amazed at what you find yourself writing!

I listen to the language of my body.

3 · LET GO OF THE PAST — AND REACH FOR THE FUTURE

CAROLINE MYSS, THE well-known medical intuitive, warns that 'biography becomes biology'.[6] Painful or traumatic memories, negative attitudes and beliefs can all become part of our physical structure. Unless we forgive and release our past, it is held in our body cells – and has a relentless impact upon our biochemistry.

A major source of illness and disease is feeling like a victim: that is, believing that someone has 'done something' to you which was quite beyond your control. ('She deserted me.' 'He was unfaithful.' 'My mother never really loved me.' 'My stepfather abused me.' 'My boss sacked me.' 'They expected too much of me.') Setting ourselves up as 'wounded victims' or martyrs does have emotional payoffs – such as wallowing in self-pity, asking for sympathy and support, or having a ready excuse for failure – but we pay a heavy price for it.

Some people pay for victimhood with their lives. Twenty years ago, I specialised in psychotherapy for people with cancer – and I was struck by how rapidly I could guess who would make a full recovery. Some clients walked into my office determined to do whatever was necessary to release the past, and reach for a positive new future; while others were just as determined to dwell on the past, and blame themselves or others for their illness. Guess who became sick again?

Being ill is often the body's way of slowly releasing emotions which we have refused to acknowledge and express. Hurt, resentment, shame, fear, grief, hatred and even love can be suppressed and 'held' in the body – gradually seeping out many months or years later as physical symptoms.

It is crucial to honour our emotions. Releasing the past does not mean denying it, or pretending that you didn't care. It means allowing the emotions to flow, to move through you as energy – without needing to defend or justify them. (Sometimes it is healing to share your feelings with a good friend or therapist – as long as they don't support you in 'victimhood'.) You also need to release any negative beliefs which *supported* those emotions, such as the belief that there is something wrong with you. *Then you need to forgive* – and release the past.

Another source of ill-health is not fulfilling your soul's destiny, or not following your Dreams. If you repeatedly ignore the promptings of your deep Self (perhaps through fear or low self-esteem), the inner conflict will eventually make you ill, anxious or depressed. Feeling trapped can also make you ill; if you feel powerless to change a situation, or to release yourself from unwanted obligations, you might 'free' yourself via an illness or accident. (A tired workaholic who had breast cancer told me she felt a strange sense of relief on hearing her diagnosis.)

If you're already ill, it is important to look honestly at why you *needed* this illness. What are the payoffs? Perhaps getting love and attention, avoiding responsibility, punishing someone, taking a break or having to put your own needs first? (And can you find *healthy* ways of meeting those needs?) Then look at the *costs* of being ill – such as discomfort, fatigue, limited activity, medical treatment, loss of income, stress on your family – and decide whether the illness is worth it.

Whatever your symptoms, you have to make a *conscious decision* to be healthy – then follow your intuition about what steps you need to take. Always focus on the future, and who you want to be – not what you have been, or what happened in the past. Give the vision of a bright and healthy future to every cell in your body.

I release the past with love – and reach for the future.

4 · HONOUR YOUR BODY'S NEEDS

THE BODY IS the temple of the soul. It is divine light moving in spirals, vibrating slowly enough to *appear* to be solid. The body has its own wisdom and intelligence, and works to maintain our health and vitality, if only we listen to and respect it. If we deny or denigrate the body, or try to 'rise above' our physical needs and desires (as religion has sometimes encouraged), it sets up an inner conflict or neurosis which makes it impossible to live in Soft Time. When we are *embodied* mystics, we live in harmony with our body and honour its needs.

Our body is constantly sending us helpful messages: slow down, keep warm, drink more water, rest more, eat more fruit, get some fresh air, stretch your muscles, take a break – and so on. We ignore these messages at our peril, since they are signposts towards positive health and prevention of dis-ease. Since everyone is unique, it is important to trust our intuition about what is right for *our* body, rather than listening to the latest fad or 'expert view' on what is good for health.

If you do become ill, consult your body wisdom about the nature of the conflict or imbalance, and what you need to do about it. (Just relax, go within – and ask to speak to your body. A response might come in the form of images, memories, fleeting thoughts or hunches. If you 'hear' something odd, such as 'Remove your electric blanket and clock radio', trust it! Your body might be very sensitive to electromagnetic fields. I was recently guided to 'Take co-enzyme supplements', which I had never heard of – but I can feel the benefit at an energy level.)

Apart from dealing with emotional stuckness or making lifestyle changes that will support your health, your body wisdom might guide you towards a healer. Western medicine still has a lot to offer – and some medics are genuine 'healers' – so don't hesitate to see a doctor if it feels right. But I believe that vibrational medicines such as homoeopathy, cranial osteopathy and flower essences will form the backbone of health care in the future, since they treat people as holistic energy systems and *support* the body rather than fighting or violating it.

Balance seems to be a universal key to good health. Research has found that older people who eat only 'health foods' and obsessively swallow vitamins do not live any longer than average – whereas those who lead a *balanced* lifestyle (three meals a day, regular bedtimes, very moderate drinking, no smoking, sensible cycles of rest and activity) live up to 11 years longer.[7]

Here are seven basic guidelines for supporting your body in creating health:

1. Eat pure and whole food, free from pesticides and other toxins.
2. Drink lots of pure water. (There is evidence that chronic dehydration might be a major root of illness,

and that it's wise to drink at least six glasses of pure water each day.[8] Tea, coffee, alcohol and salty foods all deplete our body of water.)

3. Go to bed at a regular time, and sleep for 7–8 hours.
4. Do work that you enjoy, and find meaningful. (Fatal heart attacks, for example, are least likely in those who report a high degree of job satisfaction.)
5. Spend time in nature.
6. Meditate or relax deeply every day.
7. Nurture positive emotions and supportive long-term relationships.

I trust in the wisdom of my body.

5 · INVITE BODY-SOUL FUSION

IN *ULYSSES*, JAMES Joyce wrote of a man who 'lived just a short distance from his body'. You might have come across such people – 'spacey', distant, shadowy presences who seem to hover *around* their physical body. They often speak quietly, repeat themselves a lot and appear to be in a permanent state of shock. At worst, they are quite dysfunctional in their everyday lives. In such cases, body and soul might have separated or 'de-fused' – usually the result of severe emotional or physical trauma. The soul has protected itself from potential damage by splitting off from the body, maintaining just enough contact to keep the person alive.

Although soul de-fusion is fairly uncommon, many of us experience a milder version of this, known as 'soul splitting' or 'soul loss'. We might feel numb or disconnected from life, feel rather vague or unreal, be depressed or apathetic, lack power and vitality, lose our sense of purpose or direction, suffer from memory loss, feel cut off from our body, be addictive, or simply feel that there must be 'more to life than this'. We feel disempowered, and might sense that something is missing from our lives.[9]

If you're not fully in your body – perhaps due to stressful events, too much mental work, feeling negative about your body or even meditating too much – you will not feel vital and 'alive'. According to the Huna wisdom, the body is a crucial link to your higher Self, so you'll also be cut off from your inner guidance, and from the two cornerstones of deep reality: knowing that 'I am loved' and that 'This is a safe place to be'. As William Bloom puts it, 'You cannot feel safe, you cannot feel good, unless you are fully in your body and sense that it is part of the earth'.[10]

Here are five simple ways to invite body-soul fusion:

- **Go walking in nature** – preferably barefoot on the earth – to help ground yourself in your physical body.
- **Have lots of fun** – and enjoy sensual pleasures such as hugging friends, smelling roses or lying on sun-warmed grass – so that your body feels a good place to be.
- **Love and appreciate your body.** Apologise if you have criticised or abused your body, and send it loving thoughts. (Seriously! It really makes a difference!)
- **Find a creative outlet.** Imagination and creativity give your soul a voice in the world, and so invoke body-soul fusion.
- **Breathe!** Many of us breathe shallowly into the upper chest, which suppresses emotions and bodily sensations. Breathe deep down into your belly, calmly and regularly – and for a few minutes each day, *relax* and focus on your breathing.

According to the ancient Indian tradition of Ayurvedic medicine, 'If you could live in a state of pure joy all the time, you would have the practical essence of perfect health'.[11] This requires that mind, body and spirit are balanced and integrated. It means living in deep reality – in Soft Time.

When we dwell permanently in Soft Time, limiting or negative beliefs fall away, emotions flow easily and naturally, illness and disease become unnecessary – and ageing slows down or even reverses. It is a sacred marriage of soul and body, spirit and matter. It is heaven on earth.

Heaven is here and now.

7

Home

1 · INVITE SPIRIT INTO YOUR HOME

OUR MYSTIC SELF knows that *everything* is alive and conscious, from a garden shed to a forest; that everything has a living Spirit – including our home. Yet many houses today feel 'dead' and soul-less, as if the heart has been ripped out of them. They have no warm and welcoming atmosphere, no depth of character, no song to sing. When we have lost touch with our deep Self, our home becomes just a building, an inert container for our bodily necessities and worldly goods – merely a house.

As Jane Alexander puts it, 'A real home is a place that nurtures us on every level . . . . A home with a heart embraces us when we walk through the door; we can almost feel it wrap its healing around us'.[1] Such a home has a loving, vibrant Spirit.

So how do you create a soul-ful home? Firstly, lavish your love, care, respect and attention on it. A house which is truly loved soon becomes a home. Secondly, use natural materials which resonate with the soul – such as wood, stone, terracotta, cotton, wool, cane, 'real' fires, candles, healthy plants, fresh flowers, water, sunlight and fresh air. (I fill little wicker baskets with pebbles from places such as Findhorn and New Mexico, and crystals from all over the world.) Thirdly, choose furniture which invites people to *use* it — such as comfy sofas and old pine — rather than immaculate, high-gloss designer items which say 'Keep off'.

Having an altar within your home also invokes Spirit. It needn't be large, but it provides a 'sacred space' to light a candle in celebration or prayer, or pause in thanksgiving or meditation. (For many years, my altar was on top of a blanket chest. Nowadays I use a high, deep window-ledge in our hallway which is out of reach of our toddler.) It might hold candles, family photos, small statues or sculptures, favourite quotations, incense, smudge sticks or treasured items. My own altar includes a book of Celtic prayers, a lovely Balinese temple bell,[2] a framed photo of my child's naming ceremony and a crescent-moon candle holder which was a gift from a close friend.

I also suggest that you get to know the Spirit of your home. In many traditional cultures, people still honour the spirits of the home daily at their altar, and invite guardian spirits to bless and protect their home — yet we have almost lost this mystical awareness in the West.

Once you 'know' that your home *must* have a Spirit (or angel, or deva), it is fairly easy to contact it. Ask yourself where the 'heart' of your home is, and settle down there. Go within, quiet your mind and ask to connect with the Spirit of your home. Say hello with respect, and invite it to speak to you — perhaps asking for its vision for the home, or what it expects from you. You might 'hear' words, see images, or get hunches or impressions.[3] I normally consult the Spirit of our home before making changes, such as converting our neglected dining room into a cosy snug; and I often say a cheery 'Hello' when I arrive home, and goodbye when I leave.

Every Spirit of the home is unique. The Spirit of our Rydal home feels deeply protective, quite masculine and assertive; it is like the warming presence of a bold angel. Our Cornish cottage has a very 'feminine' Spirit – ethereal, gentle, loving, welcoming and even grateful.

My home is a true sanctuary.

2 · CLEAR OUT YOUR CLUTTER

IF YOU WALK around your home, exploring cupboards, drawers, dusty shelves and hidden corners, what do you find? In all likelihood, the answer is *clutter*. Most homes are stuffed full of it; clothes you'll never wear again, books you'll never read, music you'll never listen to, piles of paper you keep meaning to sort through, clever kitchen gadgets which you've used once, unused pots and crockery, mystery boxes from when you last moved house, dead plants, unwanted gifts, half-used cosmetics, bundles of photos, pots of dried-up paint, a broken vase that you meant to glue together, a heap of unidentified whatnots that are 'sure to come in useful' . . . .

Our outer world is a mirror of our inner world – so clutter is a symbol of unfinished business, clinging to the past, stagnant energy, unwillingness to change and a belief in scarcity. According to the Huna wisdom, everything we own is connected to us by strands of energy, known as *aka* threads. Every single object either lifts our energy or depletes it – and clutter depletes it. Clutter is tiring. It scatters our thoughts, stops our own energy flowing and keeps our lives stuck. It also prevents the subtle energy (*Ch'i*) of our home from flowing freely, which affects how we feel at home, and what we attract into our lives. No wonder feng shui consultants insist that clutter-clearing is the first priority!

The general rule is: *Unless you love it or use it, it is clutter* — so chuck it out! Recycle it, give it to a friend or charity shop, sell it, burn it or simply throw it away. (And if you decide to keep it, put it where you can find it!) If it feels overwhelming to clear out the whole house, focus on one room — or even a single cupboard. Since clutter-clearing releases lots of energy, you'll probably find that you want to carry on and do more (and more) . . . .

As we clear out our homes, we are symbolically de-cluttering our psyches — releasing the old and making space for the new. It becomes easier to concentrate and think clearly, easier to focus on our priorities. It simplifies life. It feels liberating. It frees up our energy. It helps us shift into Soft Time.

Once your home is relatively free from clutter, it's easier to keep it that way. Before you bring *anything* new into the house, ask yourself whether you really want this in your sanctuary. If you really do, why not have a 'something-in-means-something-out' rule, and get rid of another item to make space for it?

One kind of clutter which is often overlooked is *communication*. Many homes are suffering from 'information overload' — from phones, faxes, mobiles, computers, TV, radio and newspapers, not to mention ordinary post and junk mail. Unless we choose to be hermits, we cannot shut it *all* out — it's an important aspect of life — but it's wise to choose what information to invite into our home, and when. Many of us are like telephone switchboards with a dozen lines left permanently open, which drowns out the subtle voice of our deep Self and keeps us in Hard Time. (Do you *have* to answer the phone whenever it rings? Do you need to read a daily paper? Or watch the news on TV? Why not gently wean yourself off, and see whether you feel more at peace? If anything important happens, you're sure to hear about it.)

Of course, it is possible to go overboard on clutter-clearing! A home which is over-cleared and over-tidied can feel empty and sterile. (My own home is full of cherubs, teddy bears and countless books, and would seem very 'cluttered' to a Zen-style minimalist.) Our homes should be well-organised and free from clutter – but filled with life.

I release the old – and create space for the new.

3 · CLEAR THE ENERGY OF YOUR HOME

EVERY HOUSE HAS an auric field, or energy field, just like we do – which can be healthy or unhealthy, flowing or blocked, sparkling or dull. And just as the human body's energy field depends on good food, clean water, hygiene, exercise, sunlight and so on, so the energy of our home is enhanced by regular and thorough cleaning, fresh air, natural light, absence of pollutants such as 'air fresheners', chemicals or sources of radiation – and a loving, joyful atmosphere created by its inhabitants.

Cleaning might not be your favourite occupation, but it becomes far more meaningful – even pleasurable and meditative – if you're aware that you are clearing the energy of your home. Since your home is a mirror of the Self, housecleaning or redecorating can be a way of releasing your past, clearing out toxic beliefs, freeing up your energy or embracing your wholeness – all while scrubbing out those kitchen cupboards, dusting shelves, wallpapering or wiping down the paintwork! (If you have a sedentary occupation, cleaning can also help to ground you back in your physical body, and balance your daily life.)

Of course, we need not be obsessive about having a clean house. Cleaning *can* become an addiction, a way of running away from one's Shadow. But if your home is filled with dust, dirt and cobwebs, or its drains are blocked, or its bins are messy and overflowing, its energy field will be clogged up – and you *will* suffer for it.

Amazingly buildings also seem to absorb complex emotional, physical and behavioural patterns from their inhabitants, holding them as energy patterns. As many traditional cultures have noted, traumatic patterns are often repeated in the same house by unrelated occupants. For example, miscarriage or infertility, breast cancer, infidelity or bankruptcy can be passed on by a house rather like genetic inheritance. For this reason, it is always wise to find out why a house is being sold before putting in an offer! (If you buy from a couple who are getting divorced, your own relationship might head into difficulties; and a 'bargain' which has been repossessed might drain your own finances.) A house also holds *your* energy patterns – so always clear your home's energy if someone has been ill, if you have had a major argument or if anything unpleasant has happened.

To clear the energy of your house – including patterns from previous occupants – always begin with a thorough clutter-clearing and cleaning. Then hold a ceremony to cleanse each room at a deeper energy level.[4] Go clockwise to each corner in turn, throwing a few grains of rock salt upwards, and a few grains downwards. (Corners tend to hold stagnant energy.) Then clap your hands, ring a bell or beat a drum to clear the energy – starting with slow, loud claps/rings/beats, and moving towards smaller, finer, faster ones – again in each corner; then repeat in the centre of the room. Affirm that only love, light and joy will now be held in this room. At the end, I always leave a lit night-light and a bowl of salt water in each room overnight.

After all this, the house should positively beam at you! You might notice that colours seem brighter, sounds seem sharper and you feel 'lighter'. You and your visitors will also tend to feel happy, relaxed and comfortable in your home. For a 'quick fix', or a regular topping-up of energy-clearing, simply open all the doors and windows for an hour, vacuum thoroughly, or burn candles and incense.

My home is sparkling with love, light and joy.

4 · LET YOUR HOME MIRROR YOUR DREAMS

OUR HOME IS a mirror of our inner Self – so by examining our home, we can learn a lot about ourselves. We can also attract or support changes in our outer lives by making changes to our home.

Examine your home as if you were an outsider, and ask yourself: 'If this house were a person, what sort of person would it be?' What impression does the house give from the outside? Does it look welcoming, formal, dark, attractive, hidden? What does the front door tell you? Does it open easily, inviting you in? What about the layout of your home? What is given most space and highest priority? Is it designed to impress others, or to enjoy? Is it well-organised or chaotic? Is it basic and functional, or does it reveal the character and passions of its inhabitants? What do the paintings on display symbolise? How does it *feel* to be in this house?

Now ask yourself: 'How would this home be different if it truly mirrored my Dreams?' If you want a committed relationship or a family, perhaps you'd have more pictures of couples or children? If you want work to be less dominant in your life, perhaps your office/study would move to the smallest room, or out of the house altogether? If you want to be more creative, perhaps you would convert the dining room into a studio? Perhaps you would redecorate the bathroom in deep rose, buy some huge fluffy towels and a wicker chair – and make it a peaceful sanctuary? Or replace that stained carpet or rickety book-shelf; or create a meditation area; or let in more light with extra windows, skylights or glass doors? Might the decor include more yellow, peach, mauve or soft white? Does the battered front door need a new coat of paint – or to be replaced? Would your Soft Time self have a real fire, more candles or lots of plump cushions?

If you are drawn to feng shui – and it is used by people and organisations all over the world – you can also use the *bagua* to help create the life of your Dreams. (*See page 239 for details.*) Decide which areas of your life need to be improved, then clutter-clear and 'enhance' the corresponding areas of your home. The *bagua* can be applied to your whole home, as well as to each room individually.[5]

For example, if you want to attract a life partner or enhance your marriage, place paired objects and images of love in the rear right of your home (or any room) – the LOVE AND MARRIAGE area of the bagua – such as pairs of candlesticks, a painting of lovers walking hand-in-hand or anything heart-shaped. Clear clutter from this area and make it look and feel warm, sensual and attractive.

Or if you've been neglecting your personal growth, focus on the front left of your home (or any room which is 'yours') – the KNOWLEDGE AND PERSONAL GROWTH area. First make it clean and tidy, then introduce symbols of growth, knowledge or spirituality such as a Buddha, an acorn, a Celtic cross, self-help books, positive affirmations, or pictures of sacred sites or 'power animals'.

In some homes, one or more areas of the *bagua* is missing due to the shape of the building. If so, it is important to 'square off' your home by including the missing area in some way. (Our home lacks a wealth area, so we placed a giant terracotta pot and plant in the missing corner, and created a path to fill in a missing edge. We also hung wind-chimes near the front door to attract good luck and prosperity.)

Ideally, the arrangement of the house should be in harmony with the *bagua* – children sleep in the children area, couples in the marriage area, a study is in the knowl-edge area, and so on. Not always practical, but worth bearing in mind!

Feng shui does seem to work. My husband was keen to compose music in his spare time – but two years after I'd bought him a gift of the necessary computer software, nothing had happened. While reorganising our sitting room, we happened to move our electric piano into the Creativity/Children area of the room. Soon after, he found he was devoting most of his spare time to writing music for my tapes for children. He had recorded several tracks before we realised that feng shui could have predicted this sudden change!

I live in the home of my Dreams.

5 · MAKE THE EARTH YOUR HOME

I AM WRITING this book just a stone's throw from Rydal Mount where William Wordsworth, poet and nature mystic, lived for 35 years. (The Wordsworth garden backs on to ours.) Is it a 'coincidence' that I am writing a book on natural mysticism here? Is this a place where spirit, nature and creativity naturally merge: an anchor point for Soft Time? I believe so — and that this is why I felt drawn to live here.

Just as our homes have a Spirit (or deva, or angel), the area which surrounds a home has a 'landscape angel' — and these Spirits have real impact upon us. If you connect with the Spirit of the place where *you* live, you might discover that you were drawn there for a higher purpose. (Likewise, your chosen holiday destinations might attract you for reasons you will not find in any glossy brochure.) A lovely way to expand our sense of 'home' is to tune into the landscape angel of the area where we live — or places we visit. Beyond that, we can also connect with the Spirit of the Earth, Gaia.[6]

Loving and cherishing our home — our bricks-and-mortar house or apartment — is important in its own right; but it is also a metaphor, a symbol of love for our greater home, Mother Earth. If we neglect our physical home, the chances are that we also feel disconnected from the planet – not to mention our deep Self.

If we see God as 'out there' (as religion might have it) or the Earth as an inert lump of rock (as science might have it), we are bound to feel lonely, yearning, separate, disconnected, homeless, alienated on Earth – and probably try to escape such feelings in unhealthy, addictive ways.

One of the joys of becoming a natural mystic is that we reconnect with our 'divine feminine' energy – with our body, with our wild Self, with nature, with the invisible realms, with the oneness – so that we no longer feel lost or displaced on Mother Earth. We know that we are Home. We plant our feet firmly on the ground. We are here. This is it. *This* is the land of milk and honey.

At a practical level, making the Earth your home might mean collecting litter while you are out walking. (Just keep a carrier bag in your pocket.) It might mean travelling more, from a desire to explore your greater home. It might mean working with pressure groups such as *Friends of the Earth*, or being more thoughtful about your own lifestyle and its impact on our shared home. It might mean envisioning the Earth as a sanctuary of beauty, peace and harmony once again; perhaps sending love and light to Gaia, or being involved in esoteric healing of the Earth at an energy level. It might mean working with landscape angels and nature spirits. Or it might simply mean feeling boundless joy and gratitude whenever you hear a blackbird sing, nestle in the limbs of a great old tree, or chance upon 'a host of golden daffodils'.

Wherever I am, I am always at Home.

Afterword

I SIT ON the soft grass in a tiny ruined chapel, a former hermitage of St Cuthbert, with broken stone walls swathed in purple clover and yellow vetch. A tall wooden cross stands before me – and way beyond it, the silhouettes of St Mary's church and the old Priory. A flock of common terns swoops and swirls in unison – dancing flecks of white against the blue sky. A warm wind whirls around me, echoing the graceful movement of the birds. I feel a deep sense of peace and contentment.

It is a glorious weekend in May. We have come to the isle of Lindisfarne on the Northumbrian coast to celebrate my birthday (and the completion of the book). I'm spending time alone in this ancient windswept chapel, notebook and pen on my lap, musing and drafting this Afterword.

Glancing towards the beach, I see my husband and toddler building a sandcastle – tiny crouched figures in the distance. My heart swells, and I recall the last time we were on an island together, playing on a sandy beach in the warm sunshine. It was on the Isle of Arran, exactly nine months ago, where this book was first conceived. (A good period for gestation!)

And so the book ends where it began – on a Holy Island. I can hardly believe it is finished. It has felt so easy and effortless to write; part of me is still waiting for the 'hard work' of writing a book to begin!

Yet I am different. Writing this book has changed me. Another year of motherhood has changed me. The Spirit of landscape has changed me. Living in Soft Time has become more and more a way of life – no longer confined to sunny beaches, sacred places, good news or occasional states of grace. It has become an everyday state of awareness. It certainly doesn't mean that my life is perfect, or that I never feel sad or angry or disturbed – but such feelings have become mere ripples on an ocean of bliss and contentment.

Gradually, 'as imperceptibly as grief', my old Hard Time habits of busyness, pressure and martyrhood have slipped away. I'm far less easily ruffled, more accepting and at peace, more aware of what really matters. I no longer feel driven to be productive. I value my time in a new and different way. I can (and do) slip back into Hard Time, but I spot it more quickly nowadays – sometimes within moments – and usually return to Soft Time, like a homing pigeon, almost automatically. My former 'strategies' for shifting into Soft Time have become an inseparable part of how I live and who I am.

Rather like misty memories of long hot summers of child-hood, my days now pass in a timeless haze of 'boundless love', joy and creativity. Every day feels like a holiday: feeding the ducks, splashing in puddles, dancing in the open air, gazing at the moon and stars, walking the fells, changing nappies, clearing up messes, chasing and cuddling and laughing – and doing work that I truly love.

And now that the book is finished, I look forward to the long summer months ahead: time to relax with family and friends, catch up on novels and poetry, paint a few pictures, consider new projects or just sit and 'moodle' more – enjoying the pure bliss of Soft Time.

As the tide floods in to isolate the tiny chapel, I cross the watery sands and seaweed-covered rocks to re-join my family, and collect shells to decorate the sandcastle. I am filled with gratitude. Life feels infinitely rich and full and precious – brimming with wonder and possibility.

> *Deep peace, a soft white dove to you . . .*
> *Deep peace of the running wave to you,*
> *Deep peace of the flowing air to you,*
> *Deep peace of the quiet earth to you,*
> *Deep peace of the sleeping stones to you.*
> *Deep peace, deep peace!*
>
> Celtic blessing

Acknowledgements

My love and thanks to:

- Gill, Judy and everyone at Piatkus for your positive approach and loving support;
- My parents – for reading the original manuscript with such care, for your helpful suggestions and (most of all) for your constant love and support;
- My soul-sister Trina – for your useful comments on early drafts, and simply for being 'you';
- All of the thousands of LIVING MAGICALLY workshop attenders over the past ten years, who have given and taught me more than you will ever know;
- Susie Thomas, my workshop assistant and friend of many years, whose bubbling joy and immense generosity of

spirit are always an inspiration and delight;

- Celeste and my team of guides in the unseen realms, for your loving guidance and inspiration; to Bartholomew (and Joy Ballas-Beeson) who foresaw me writing this book many years ago; to Orin (and Sanaya Roman) for all that you have given me; and to Isis, my 'highest teacher';
- The Spirits of place who have filled and inspired me – in particular, the landscape angels of Rydal, the Lake District, Cornwall and the Isle of Arran, and the spirit of our family home, Undermount;
- John, whose invaluable comments and insights helped to shape the book, and who cared for Kieran so that I could have a little more writing time. Thank you for your endless love and support – and for all the fun, laughter and joy we share;
- And, of course, to Kieran – for the 'boundless love', giggles and delight, and for teaching me so much about the art of living in Soft Time.

Notes

PART ONE

Prelims

1. Rumi (transl. by Kabir Helminski), *Love is a Stranger* (Threshold, 1993), page 62.

Chapter One

1. Mihaly Csikszentmihalyi, *Flow – The Psychology of Happiness* (Rider, 1992).
2. Viktor Frankl, *Man's Search for Meaning* (Washington Square Press, 1985).

Chapter Two

1. See Joseph Chilton Pearce, *Magical Child* (Penguin/ Plume, 1992), page 193.

2. ibid., pages 127–137.
3. Clarissa Pinkola Estés, *Women Who Run with the Wolves* (Rider, 1992).
4. e.g. see Theodor Roszak, Mary E. Gomes and Allen D. Kramer (eds), *Ecopsychology* (Sierra Club Books, 1995) and Theodore Roszak, *The Voice of the Earth* (Simon & Schuster, 1992).
5. John O'Donohue, *Anam Cara: Spiritual Wisdom from the Celtic World* (Bantam Press, 1997).
6. See Hunter Davies, *A Walk Around The Lakes* (Dent, 1980/93).
7. Henry David Thoreau, *Thoughts from Walden Pond* (Pomegranate, 1998), page 31.
8. A term borrowed from Matthew Fox, *Whee! We, Wee: All the Way Home* (Bear & Co, 1981).

Chapter Three

1. Taken from 'The Kingdom of God' (1913).
2. Taken from *Little Gidding*.
3. See my self-help tape on 'Healing Your Inner Adolescent'.
4. Jean Liedloff, *The Continuum Concept* (Penguin/Arkana, 1989), page 43; first published 1975.
5. See Deborah Jackson, *Three in a Bed* (Bloomsbury, 1990).

Chapter Four

1. Matthew Fox, *The Coming of the Cosmic Christ* (HarperCollins, San Francisco, 1988), page 44.
2. Quote in Matthew Fox, *Original Blessing* (Bear & Co., Santa Fe, New Mexico, 1983), page 59.
3. i.e., Pantheism – see Matthew Fox, *The Coming of the Cosmic Christ* (HarperCollins, San Francisco, 1988), page 50.
4. Translated by Man-Ho Kwok, Martin Palmer and Jay Ramsay, *Tao Te Ching* (Element, 1994), page 141.
5. See my earlier book, *Stepping into The Magic* (Piatkus, 1993).
6. Serge Kahili King, *Urban Shaman* (Simon & Schuster, 1990).
7. Pali Jae Lee and Koko Willis, *Tales from the Night Rainbow* (Night Rainbow Publishing Co., Honolulu, 1988), page 19.
8. ibid., page 59.
9. ibid., page 60.
10. John O'Donohue, *Anam Cara: Spiritual Wisdom from the Celtic World* (Bantam, 1997), page 271.
11. Matthew Fox, *The Coming of the Cosmic Christ* (HarperCollins, San Francisco, 1988), page 58.
12. Barry Lopez, *Of Wolves and Men* (Macmillan, New York, 1978), page 285.
13. e.g. see Ervin Laszlo, *The Whispering Pond* (Element, 1996).
14. Amit Goswami, *The Self-Aware Universe* (Tarcher/Putnam, 1995), page 50.
15. Quoted in Matthew Fox, *Original Blessing* (Bear & Co., Santa Fe, New Mexico, 1983), page 35.

16. From 'New Age', in Jay Ramsay (ed.) *Transformation: The Poetry of Spiritual Consciousness* (Rivelin Grapheme Press, 1988), page 92.
17. John O'Donohue, *Anam Cara: Spiritual Wisdom from the Celtic World* (Bantam, 1997), page 120.

PART TWO

Chapter 1

1. See Karen Kingston, *Clear Your Clutter with Feng Shui* (Piatkus, 1998) for an excellent analysis of what clutter means, how it affects us and what to do about it.
2. I learnt this version of the well-known saying from Serge Kahili King.
3. Richard Carlson and Joseph Bailey, *Slowing Down to the Speed of Life* (Hodder & Stoughton, 1997).
4. See my earlier book *Living Magically* (Piatkus, 1991) for further details.
5. If this feels impossible, it's well worth seeing a good psychotherapist for a while.
6. A term I learnt from Bartholomew, channelled by Joy Ballas-Beeson.

Chapter Two

1. This inner journey is available on my self-help tape, *Healing or Releasing a Relationship*.

Chapter Three

1. At a recent workshop of mine, I asked 90 participants to think of a favourite childhood memory. Then I asked

how many of those memories involved being in nature; 75 per cent put up their hands.

2. Randall Colton Rolfie, quoted in Linda Crispell Aronson, *Big Spirits, Little Bodies* (A.R.E. Press, Virginia, 1995), page 59.
3. A more positive term for 'unconditional love', taken from Aronson (1995).
4. My earlier books give more information about past lives and reincarnation.
5. See Carol Bowman, *Children's Past Lives* (Element, 1998).

Chapter Four

1. Nick Williams, *The Work We Were Born to Do* (Element, 1999).
2. Diane Fassel, *Working Ourselves to Death* (Harper, San Francisco, 1990), page 2.
3. Richard Carlson, *Don't Worry, Make Money* (Hodder & Stoughton, 1998), pages 93–4.
4. Declan Treacy, *Clear Your Desk* (Arrow, 1998).
5. Jane Roberts, *The Nature of Personal Reality* (Prentice Hall, New York, 1987), page 35.
6. Aviva Gold, *Painting from the Source* (Thorsons, 1998), pages 132–4.

Chapter Five

1. I believe that money problems are often due to vows of poverty taken in past lifetimes which need to be released. See my earlier book, *Stepping into the Magic*, or my tape-set on *Creating Prosperity* for more details.

Chapter Six

1. Deepak Chopra, *Ageless Body, Timeless Mind* (Rider, 1993), page 5.
2. Carl & Stephanie Simonton, *Getting Well Again* (Bantam, 1978).
3. Deepak Chopra, *Quantum Healing* (Bantam, 1989), pages 122–5.
4. Brandon Bays, *The Journey* (Thorsons, 1999).
5. Deepak Chopra, *Perfect Health* (Bantam, 1990), page 10.
6. Caroline Myss, *Anatomy of the Spirit* (Bantam, 1997).
7. Deepak Chopra, *Perfect Health* (Bantam, 1990), page 192.
8. Water also helps to clear toxins from the body, and to integrate left and right brain.
9. See my self-help tape on *Soul Retrieval* for further details.
10. From notes for a forthcoming book by William Bloom on Body-Soul Harmonics.
11. Deepak Chopra, *Perfect Health* (Bantam, 1990), page 110.

Chapter Seven

1. Jane Alexander, *Spirit of the Home* (Thorsons, 1998), pages 2–3.
2. Obtained from Karen Kingston – see suggested reading.
3. For further information, see Jane Alexander's book above; or William Bloom, *Working with Angels, Fairies & Nature Spirits* (Piatkus, 1998).
4. For more details, see Karen Kingston, *Creating Sacred*

Space with Feng Shui (Piatkus, 1996) and Denise Linn, *Sacred Space* (Rider, 1995).

5. For more information, see Terah Kathryn Collins, *The Western Guide to Feng Shui* (Hay House, 1996), William Spear, *Feng Shui Made Easy* (Thorsons, 1995) – or countless other books.

6. The devic stream of consciousness (which includes angels and nature spirits) is always in Soft Time. Connecting with the angelic realms helps to balance us and expand our awareness. We cannot do it from Hard Time, so don't try too hard! Just relax, stay calm and imagine your consciousness drifting up to finer and finer levels – then call in the Angel. Let go of any expectations, and be open to any subtle impressions, feelings or images. For more details, see William Bloom's excellent book, *Working with Angels, Fairies & Nature Spirits* (Piatkus, 1998).

Suggested Reading

I've deliberately kept the book list to a bare minimum of 25 recent or long-standing favourites of mine. For me, all of these books are deeply inspiring, thought-provoking, practical, informative and/or consciousness-shifting.

If you love reading, these books will lead you on to others – and there are longer bibliographies in my books *Living Magically* (Piatkus, 1991) and *Stepping into the Magic* (Piatkus, 1993). There are also references to many other wonderful books in the text and footnotes of *Pure Bliss*.

Jane Alexander, *Spirit of the Home* (Thorsons, 1998)
Melody Beattie, *The Language of Letting Go* (Hazelden Foundation, 1990)
Polly Berrien Berends, *Whole Child/Whole Parent* (Harper &

Row, 1983/1987)

William Bloom, *Working with Angels, Fairies and Nature Spirits* (Piatkus, 1998)

Sarah Ban Breathnach, *Simple Abundance* (Bantam, 1996)

Julia Cameron, *The Artist's Way: A Course in Discovering and Recovering Your Creative Self* (Pan, 1995)

Richard Carlson and Joseph Bailey, *Slowing Down to the Speed of Life* (Hodder & Stoughton, 1998)

Deepak Chopra, *Quantum Healing* (Bantam, 1989)

Terah Kathryn Collins, *The Western Guide to Feng Shui* (Hay House, 1996)

Clarissa Pinkola Estés, *Women Who Run with the Wolves* (Rider, 1992)

Matthew Fox, *The Reinvention of Work* (HarperCollins, 1994)

Amit Goswami, *The Self-Aware Universe: How Consciousness Creates the Material World* (Tarcher/Putnam, 1995)

Enid Hoffman, *Huna: A Beginner's Guide* (Whitford, 1976)

Serge Kahili King, *Urban Shaman* (Fireside, 1990)

Karen Kingston, *Creating Sacred Space with Feng Shui* (Piatkus, 1996)

John O'Donohue, *Anam Cara: Spiritual Wisdom from the Celtic World* (Bantam, 1997)

Carol Orsborn, *Enough Is Enough* (New World Library, 1992)

Jay Ramsay, *Kingdom of the Edge: Poems for the Spirit* (Element, 1999)

Stephan Rechtschaffen, *Timeshifting* (Rider, 1996)

Sanaya Roman, *Living with Joy* (H. J. Kramer, 1986)

Sanaya Roman and Duane Packer, *Creating Money* (H. J. Kramer, 1988)

Theodor Roszak, Mary E. Gomes and Ellen D. Kanner,

Ecopsychology: Restoring the Earth, Healing the Mind (Sierra Club Books, 1995)

Norman Shealy and Caroline Myss, *The Creation of Health* (Stillpoint Publishing, 1988/1993)

Rupert Sheldrake, *The Rebirth of Nature* (Rider, 1990)

Joyce and Barry Vissell, *Models of Love: The Parent–Child Journey* (Ramira, 1986)

🌿

GILL EDWARDS

For free brochure/newsletter with details of Gill's current workshops, books, self-help tapes etc., please contact:

Living Magically
Fisherbeck Mill
Old Lake Road
Ambleside
Cumbria
LA22 0DH
Tel: (015394) 31943 / Fax: (015394) 31946

Website: www.livingmagically.co.uk